THE HEART OF EUROPE

The Heart of Europe

Denis de Rougemont
and
Charlotte Muret

DUELL, SLOAN AND PEARCE
NEW YORK

Third printing

PRINTED IN THE UNITED STATES OF AMERICA

To the Swiss People who are struggling today as did their ancestors of old to keep their country free and true to its mission we dedicate this book, our small contribution to their great task.

Honneur et Fidélité.

—Device on the Flag of the Swiss Regiments in Foreign Service.

Un pour tous et tous pour un.

—Swiss Federal Motto.

Walled towns, stored arsenals and armories, goodly races of horses, chariots of war, elephants, ordnance, artillery and the like; all this is but a sheep in a lion's skin, except the breed and disposition of the people be stout and warlike.

—FRANCIS BACON.

CONTENTS

PREFACE

This volume is neither a guide book nor a history of Switzerland. It is not even an exhaustive study of that country in any of its aspects. It is a description of how one people has managed to remain free and diverse yet united.

We believe that Federalism in the sense of such a union of diversities is the most vital necessity of the future, and that all who care for freedom and democracy should realize it. This belief has led us to describe Switzerland as the illustration and example of a truly Federal State. Swiss history, Swiss character, the political and economic structure of the country, its intellectual life, its army, are discussed from this point of view.

The book itself is a product of "Federalism," for its authors are unlike in almost everything; one of us was born and bred in Switzerland, the other in the American Far West; one of us is conservative, the other progressive. We are different in age, experience, and culture, yet our collaboration has been complete, and our work is the result of a union of mind and thought which has brought joy and profit to us both.

We wish to thank here all those who have helped us with their advice, information, and encouragement. May the book give them some part of the pleasure which the writing of it has given us.

Charlotte T. Muret
Denis de Rougemont

THE HEART OF EUROPE

I. CHALLENGING PARADOXES

WHEN you read the newspapers, you find that Switzerland is only a little country which has so far had the good luck not to attract much attention. But when you read history, you find that Switzerland is perhaps the formula for the only possible European future. That is why it seems opportune today to describe this solution to modern problems, which, though on a small scale, has the immense advantage of being actually in existence, and of having survived six and one-half centuries of history.

The following pages set forth a series of observations which have a direct bearing on the urgent problems common to all democracies of today. They are not propaganda, for propaganda is unnecessary between friends, and the good will that unites America and Switzerland is of the most solid and enduring kind. It is founded on a common ideal which the present world crisis can only deepen and render more self-conscious.

Though friendship is born of instinctive sympathy, it develops only through ever-closer knowledge. That is why this book has been written, for a curious anomaly exists in regard to Switzerland in this country; Americans love it, but for the most part they know nothing about it. They accept it on the faith of publicity slogans as the land of alps and cows, of hotels and fine watches. A few might add that it is a little country lying between Germany and France, an old democracy, and the home of the Red Cross and the League of Nations.

All these things are true enough, but they give no idea of the real country, of its deep and significant organic unity. The Swiss reality is far more complex than Americans in general, or even the Swiss themselves, know.

In examining Switzerland we will describe and comment, but we will refrain as far as possible from political speculation. The history of the twentieth century shows that there is nothing more murderous than political abstractions, and perhaps the time is at hand when men will refuse to be killed for "isms," for supposedly irreconcilable causes, which are soon revealed as having been accomplices in the slaughter committed in their names.

We will therefore try in this little book to present living facts, not theories nor such dead data as statistics. We will try to show you *à propos* of Switzerland that contemporary reality can only have significance when seen in the perspective of a long tradition.

Switzerland is the oldest democracy in the world, and it is the last one surviving in Europe. The foun-

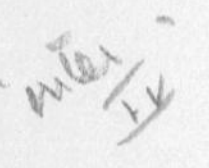

dation of the Confederacy dates back to the first of August, 1291. Thus the Swiss State has had 650 years of uninterrupted autonomous life. A glance at the map of Europe shows that it is now the last free state in the midst of that continent. Two other continental states are still nominally independent at this writing: the Swedish monarchy and the Portuguese dictatorship, but they are countries which lie on the borders of Europe, and they have been spared so far largely because they are remote.

The Helvetian Confederation, a strange combination of paradoxes lying at the very heart of Europe, has for centuries incarnated some of the most important lessons, both positive and negative, which democracy must learn today, if it is to survive. These lessons have emerged slowly during the course of a complex history. They have become clear only in the light of the present conflict. This appalling upheaval, this overthrow not only of all our political creations but of our sentimental illusions, was needed to make us begin to see among such ruins the solid ground, the basic structure on which we may hope to rebuild.

Switzerland is indeed the most paradoxical of countries, and each of its paradoxes implies a question, the answer to which is of vital importance to every democracy in the world. The mere enumeration of them suggests the challenge which this little country presents to the world of the twentieth century:

First, in its narrow territory—one of the smallest in

Europe—Switzerland has concentrated and synthesized all the diversities of Europe itself.

In the central mountain range of the Gothard rise four great rivers: the Rhine, which waters Germany and Holland; the French Rhône; the Italian Po; and, with the Inn, the Danube, which flows through Austria and the Balkans. Thus in the heart of Switzerland the French, the German, and the Mediterranean civilizations meet. Federal laws are published in four languages, German, French, Italian, and Romanche, and each of the German cantons, 17 out of the 22 little states which form the Confederation, speaks a different dialect.

If you were to cross Switzerland in the express train from Basel to Locarno you would pass in the course of four hours through all the climates and all the varieties of culture in Europe, from the Nordic pine forests to the orange groves and palm trees of the Italian lakes, through a temperate and densely peopled plateau, and through the desert zone of the Alps.

Is it this very diversity, recognized, cultivated, and harmonized, which has given Switzerland its stability?

Second, Switzerland is both the most advanced democracy of Europe and the country most deeply attached to tradition.

In the old Catholic regions such as the cantons of Lucerne and Fribourg, an aristocracy of feudal origins still rules in fact, though not in law, over the agricultural villages which cluster about its castles.

In the small cantons of the central Alpine region the laws are voted and the magistrates elected by the body of the citizens assembled in the public square.

In the larger cities such as Zurich and Geneva a patrician bourgeoisie, liberal and Anglophile, enriched by industry and banking, maintains a social hierarchy as rigid as any in the world (much like that which exists in the Boston of Beacon Street). But equality is absolute as soon as we enter the political domain. Money does not lead to public honors, the magistrates and the bureaucracy are incorruptible, and the son of a peasant has a much better chance of being president of the Confederation than the son of a family whose nobility dates back a thousand years.

Moreover, Switzerland is the only democracy—or, indeed, nation—in the world which has dared to entrust to each man his gun, his ammunition, and all his military equipment in peacetime—a striking proof of the civic maturity of the Swiss, and of the confidence which the State feels in its citizens.

Does Switzerland owe its sturdy progressiveness to the vitality of its age-old traditions?

Third, Switzerland is at once the most pacific country in Europe and the most highly armed.

Pacific it is, for since the time of the Treaties of Vienna in 1815 its absolute and perpetual neutrality has been solemnly recognized by the great powers as being "in the interests of all Europe." Pacific, because in addition to renouncing all voluntary participation in any armed conflict, it has been the refuge of the military and civilian victims of war, and because it has founded the International Red Cross and the agency for the relief of prisoners, institutions created for the purpose of bringing a little human peace into the organized massacres of our civilization. Lastly it is pacific because by harmonizing in one federation three civilizations, elsewhere at war, two religions traditionally antagonistic, four languages and an unknown number of "races," it has deserved to be called "a Europe reconciled with itself."

Yet on the other hand the same Treaty of Vienna which guaranteed to Switzerland its perpetual neutrality laid upon the Confederation the responsibility for defending its neutrality and independence by its own efforts. That is why Switzerland, with a population of four and one-half million inhabitants, keeps up an army of 600,000 men, half of whom have been permanently mobilized since September, 1939.

Nowhere in Europe, not even in Germany, is the military spirit more highly developed than in the Swiss population. Nowhere is the army to a like degree the possession of the whole people. Nowhere else is the citizen so completely fused in the soldier, on the day of danger. Lastly, nowhere else had a preparation for modern warfare and a defensive organization against a Blitzkrieg been so minutely prepared over a period of ten years before the present war.

Does Switzerland owe the peace which it still enjoys to the fact that it is proportionately the best-armed democracy in the world?

Fourth, Switzerland is both the seat of almost all the international institutions of Europe and the country the most passionately attached to its local institutions.

How is it that all nations have agreed to locate the site of the League of Nations, of the International Labor Bureau, of the Bank for International Settlements, of the Universal Postal Union and of about ninety other analogous institutions, in Switzerland? How explain that Switzerland is the most "international" country of Europe, while on the other hand it is here that local spirit is still most active, that the communes have the greatest amount of autonomy, that each canton forms a separate State, with its parliament, its popular assembly, its executive power, its code of laws which differ from those of the neighboring cantons, and its customs, private and public, jealously and resolutely preserved? How can this almost medieval agglomeration of local, often narrow, particularisms have given birth to some of the most widely European minds of the continent, and to a whole cohort of international negotiators?

Is it possible that to be deeply rooted in local realities is the essential condition which allows a people to look serenely beyond its own frontiers?

Fifth, the natural resources of Switzerland are very limited, yet the standard of living of its people is one of the highest in Europe.

Switzerland has concentrated its activity on the economic pursuits in which it has had the greatest natural advantages, and in those fields it has exhibited an energy and an ingenuity which have made its special national products, chocolate and cheese, locomotives, electrical machinery and watches, synonymous with quality. Though it has no raw materials, Switzerland is proportionally the greatest exporting country in the world.

Inevitably, then, Switzerland has been a part of the larger European and even world economy. It has never flirted with economic nationalism, and it has profited thereby.

Does the success of the Swiss economy constitute a mere memorial to the principles of free trade and specialization, or is it suggestive for the future?

Sixth, historically Switzerland is the last remnant of medieval Europe, but it may also become the first model of a federal Europe of tomorrow.

In the thirteenth century, the passage of the Gothard was opened in the midst of the Alps, in the very spot where the four great European rivers rise. It became at once the main artery of the Holy Roman Empire, for it was the pass which connected those two separate halves of the Empire, the North and the South. The Swiss were entrusted with its defense in the name of the Emperor, and in the common interest of the neighboring peoples. Such is the origin of the Swiss Confederation. From that time on, the Swiss were a sort of European militia, and their country was recognized as free because it was an "Imperial Domain," not a feudal state like the others. This special function, this mission, gave Switzerland a sort of extra-territorial status in Europe, from which came the perpetual neutrality later bestowed on the Confederation by the spontaneous agreement of the Powers.

The Holy Roman Empire has disappeared, but the Swiss still mount guard vigilantly over their bastion, which is both a vital artery and a symbol. They hold the keys of the vanished Empire. They preserve the idea of a confederated Europe, and practice it within their frontiers. They are still the predestined guardians of the values and institutions common to all the peoples of the continent.

If, as we believe, the Holy Roman Empire was a first incarnation of the federal idea, preserved by the Swiss cantons alone in all our torn and divided western world, and if the only conceivable hope for us lies in a peace where nations will renounce the "divine" right of sovereignty which they have unjustifiably assumed—can we not hope that tomorrow, or day-after-tomorrow, Switzerland may become the first small seed of a federated Europe?

A seed. The image is appropriate to the size of our country. A seed is always the consummation, the end of an old life; but if it is fertilized and allowed slowly to mature, it may become the promise of a new one.

Switzerland, at present encircled by the Axis powers, is a living refutation, a concrete and indisputable denial, of the totalitarian ideal. The Swiss have never asked for any other "living space" than liberty. By its very existence Switzerland proves that several races can live together in harmony, and on a footing of scrupulous equality; that it is possible to unite, in a freedom of diversity, various languages, various modes of life, and that this union is far more truly human than the enforced unity of the dictatorships. By its very existence it refutes the racial and nationalistic theories. Lastly, by its very existence Switzerland is a permanent manifesto against totalitarian war, totalitarian arrogance, and the insane superstition of the *Kolossal* which is at the root of the totalitarian evil.

Although there was a period when it was the strongest military power in Europe, Switzerland has chosen to remain small in order to remain human. It has chosen to remain diverse in order to preserve concrete liberties. It has refused to believe that Man's reasons for living could be conquered by force, and yet it has been ready to remain at arms in order to defend its own existence "in the interests of all Europe," according to its particular mission. It owes to its army its continued existence at the present moment.

This example, this reality, this hope, is worthy of consideration by those who seek to understand the present era.

The conventional picture of Switzerland can be summed up in the well-known line: "The Swiss peasant milks his cow and lives in peace."

But we do not think that a genuine realism consists in taking only the pettiest aspects of life seriously. If Switzerland can celebrate in this very year the 650th anniversary of its liberties, it must certainly be because it has meant more in the world than an idyllic picture-postcard scene.

Victor Hugo in one of his outbursts of irresponsible prophecy was once guilty of the following line—no less well known than the one quoted above:

"In history Switzerland will have the last word."

We may smile, but we may also wonder whether the reality of Switzerland, which lies between the two extremes of a sordid realism and a millennial vision, does not represent for our century the last conceivable hope of a peace which would not be heavenly, perhaps, but which would be human. This is the question that we will attempt to answer.

II. THE FACE OF SWITZERLAND

IN order to see the unity of Switzerland we must look at it from a height. On the level of the lakes and fields, the land is enclosed and divided, the horizons are close, shut in by hills or mountain barriers. But if we climb, as in an aeroplane, the country takes shape. The natural depressions become evident, and a long plateau, like the arc of a circle, hollows itself between the dark walls of the Jura and the vast frozen waves which are the parallel chains of the Alps. Rising higher, we see appear, wrapped in a golden haze, the two extremities of this arc, two streaks of pale blue, Lake Leman on the French side and the Lake of Constance on the German. To the north, beyond the ribbon of the Rhine, the Black Forest and the Balloon of the Vosges prolong the undulations of the Jura. To the south on the other side of the Alps the plains of Lombardy fade into a rose and ocher dust. Is that a mirage that we glimpse, or is it the sea?

Below us, the summits of the two great Alpine ranges, floating above the earth between the deep folds of their transverse valleys, shine serenely brilliant. We are flying over the roof of Europe.

Almost at the top of the vast semi-circle formed by the corrugations of the Alps, from the Mediterranean to the plains of Austria and Croatia, in the center of Switzerland, the parallel ranges meet and intertwine into a chaotic mass. Four main valleys issue from this mass, down which the four rivers flow, hollowing out in the heart of this granitic turmoil a vast cross, like a symbolic seal. To the north towards the Atlantic go the waters of the Rhine, to the west and the Mediterranean the waters of the Rhône, to the south and the Adriatic the waters of the Ticino, which will become the Po, to the east and the Balkan plains the waters of the Inn, which through the Danube will flow into the Black Sea.

The middle of this cross of rivers is cut by a road which we see climbing up to a remote lake, then going down towards northern Italy. A long train disappears into the mountain, and reappears a moment later, farther on. This is the only spot in the Alps where a single road and a single tunnel join the northern and the southern worlds.

This cross of rivers, this roof of Europe, this master-knot of the Alps and unique passage is the St. Gothard. It is one of the most symbolic places in the world, the heart of Switzerland, and also the heart of the continent.

We will leave this mystery for the moment. It is enough to know that it exists, and that, however unaware of it most people may be, like a master-thought it dominates the multiple daily life of this country, with its varied landscapes and history. Let us go back to the life of men. By a typically Swiss contrast we drop from the sublime to the dapper.

In the two days of a circular trip we can visit all of Switzerland, but in that time we will have seen a kind of synopsis of Europe, of its landscapes, its climates, its crops, its customs. Suppose we enter Switzerland by Basel, an old city of the German Renaissance, built on an elbow of the Rhine, whose outlying districts touch Germany on the north and France on the west. We leave the international sleeping car for one of the Swiss "express" trains which stop every half hour—for here everything is close at hand, and each city is a center, and deserves a visit. We must travel third class, like everybody else in the country save officers, commercial travelers and the newly rich. For unless you have the courage to travel on foot, the best way to see a new country is to mix with the movable population of local trains.

The mere examination of our third class coach gives an idea of certain typical Swiss traits. The baggage-rack and benches are of a highly varnished yellow wood, like that of schoolroom desks, and just as in a schoolroom we are warned at once of a certain number of things we are not to do. A sign on every window sill repeats peremptorily: "Nicht hinaus lehnen—Ne pas se pencher au dehors—E pericoloso sporgersi." No penalty is attached to the rule, as it would be in America, for the authorities trust in the sense of discipline of the Swiss citizen—and it would be unforgivable to disobey in three languages! Yet, since you are a stranger, let us take advantage of one of the rare moments when the "controller" in his blue uniform is neither coming nor going, to disobey and lean out. You run no risk of a cinder in your eye, for all the trains are electrified and you will breathe the pure air which Rousseau called the "air of liberty," and which is like the physical soul of the country.

Our fellow travelers are talking of the weather, as people do everywhere, yet not exactly in the same way, for here the conversation is serious. Every Swiss is something of a meteorologist, or at least an experienced connoisseur in the meaning of the clouds and the three kinds of wind which blow in each region. These are the cold, clear northwest wind, the Bise, or the rainy South wind, which is simply called *the* wind, or the local breeze, whose name is always in dialect—whether it be the Joran, which, falling from the Jura with sudden savagery, scatters and sinks the boats on the lakes, or the Foehn of the Alps, whose hot breath brings storm and avalanche. To talk of the weather is a necessity in a place where everything has to be wrested from a violent, changeable and often hostile nature, which dominates daily life with its vagaries, yet is also, thanks to the tourist trade, one of the great sources of wealth.

When your neighbors have exhausted the subject of the weather, they will, if they are masculine, fall to talking of their military service. We will hear them on that subject later; just now they have too much to say, and we to see.

The train is passing through the high valleys of the Jura. Secret valleys, darkened by stern pines massed in regular ranks along the hill-tops. In this austerely romantic setting the villages are prosaic, with their great gray houses of unornamented stone, protected often against the winter wind by a sort of jacket of shingles or tin. There are a few factories, a few farm houses. This is the land of the watchmakers. It is here that Hans Andersen wrote some of his loveliest fairy tales, and here, too, the First International was started.

We pass from one to another of these valleys through deep gorges and frequent tunnels. Here is one longer than the rest from which we issue suddenly into the full sunlight, and blink, dazzled, before a vast space bathed in bright haze. What is that silvery blue mirage which rises full in the sky to the south? Generally the traveler from abroad rubs his eyes and asks his neighbor if those are really the Alps. It is indeed they. From the Mont Blanc to the Range of the Gothard like a thin line of clouds they stretch in an immense semi-circle between earth and sky. Between the slopes of the Jura, down which we are now moving obliquely, and that horizon, stretch the wide undulations of the Swiss plateau, in long parallel lines of black and blue forests, of meadows and woods and wheat fields. We glimpse here and there the top of a steeple or a tower belonging to some city hidden in a hollow.

The impression of immensity given by the landscape results not from its actual size, but from its proportion, its broad architecture, which is reflected in the still waters of a long lake which we are nearing—that of Neuchâtel.

Leaving behind us the dark gateway of the Nordic Jura we have changed worlds in a few minutes. At our feet terraced vineyards fall away, and a few slow-moving sails drift birdlike on the unbroken surface of the lake, whose far shores have an almost Tuscan warmth. The vision of the Alps floats on the horizon.

Let us wander on the quays of Neuchâtel, this little city built of yellow stone. The scene is animated by the flight of many gulls and pigeons, and the odor of the lake invites to a leisure at once pleasant and melancholy. Here we are at the confines of German romanticism on the one hand and of the easygoing south on the other. There are few passersby in the streets, and those we see are unhurried. On the open terraces of the cafés sit students and young girls who speak every tongue in the world, for Neuchâtel is a university town, and it is full of schools. There is a sense of holiday—of having plenty of time. The houses are clean, and the pastry shops fascinating. Many writers, André Gide among them, have said that they dreamed of ending their days in this city.

A few kilometers to the east of Neuchâtel we cross a river which is the linguistic frontier, and we enter Germanic Switzerland. At once the houses have a different aspect. The large farms of the canton of Berne are undoubtedly the finest in the world. Set in dazzlingly green valleys—one would think that each blade of grass had been newly varnished that morning—shaded by giant oaks, deeply overhanging eaves spread above long buildings of white stone, half covered with carved woodwork. Along the galleries which surround them, in front of each small-paned window with its lace curtains, bright geraniums glow. The typical farm is divided into three adjoining parts: the peasant's dwelling, the stable, and the barn. In the sheds you will find old-fashioned wooden carts with ladders, side-by-side with modern American tractors. In the house there are nearly always carved cupboards several hundred years old, a collection of pewter pots and dishes, diplomas of gymnastic or sharp-shooting societies framed and hung on the wall, and also a bathroom and a grand piano. These are "upper middle class" peasants whose like could probably be found only in Scandinavia.

Forests, valleys, meadows, and everywhere white roads going up and down hill, skirting a field, crossing a river on a wooden-roofed bridge. Little by little, the forest becomes a park. Modest little town houses painted green or pink appear, grouped in colonies (Siedlungen) in an open glade or prairie. These are the suburbs of Berne, which is not called the capital, but the "Federal City," a distinction felt to be important by all Swiss people.

Coming up from the station at Berne, which is filled with skiers or Alpine climbers, you will find yourself at the entrance of one of the most remarkable streets in Europe. The Middle Ages, the German Renaissance, traces of the French eighteenth century in the decoration of its façades combine to form an harmonious and powerful architectural ensemble. The four-story houses are sheltered by projecting eaves and heavily supported by oblique buttresses and low-vaulted arcades. Under the tunnel of the arcades moves a crowd half peasant, half bourgeois. Here, as in the countryside, all the first floor windows are gay with pots of geraniums, and between them, little red cushions, on which the townspeople lean comfortably while they watch the evening spectacle of the street.

It is a broad, paved street, in which a double row of stone slabs still marks the carriage-way, between the tracks of the street cars. The vista is broken by two large square towers painted with frescoes and bearing "surprise" clocks. A golden giant standing under the pointed eaves of the tower moves at noon, and strikes a bell with twelve blows of his hammer, while the good Emperor Joseph and his knights come out of a recess, pass by, bowing, and re-enter the wall, to the great joy of the children and their nurses, who wait eagerly for this daily sight. A series of fountains surmounted by statues complete the fantastic yet wonderfully human aspect of this street. These fountains consist of large round basins, in the midst of which rise carved stone columns painted in vivid blue, red and gold. One of these columns carries a banneret[1] in armor, another an ogre busily devouring fat little children, a third, blind Justice, and a fourth, a bear with a golden helmet, holding a banner. The bear is the totem of Berne, from which the city drew its name. It figures on the city coat-of-arms, on cakes and sticks of chocolate, on gingerbread cookies where a white sugar bear sticks out a pink tongue, and it is at Berne that the bear has his official residence in the famous pit which can be seen at the end of the main street.

This pit is a deep arena surrounded by a low fence, in which two families of big brown bears roam about with deceptive ponderousness, and are copiously supplied with carrots and peanuts by a crowd of guests and affectionate friends. What other city in the world has kept such a living symbol of its peculiar genius? All the strength of Berne—once, like Venice, a powerful state—is symbolized in the apparent

[1] The standard-bearer.

slowness of an animal which in fact excels at seizing its prey without a single useless move. Watch them catching the carrots which the children throw them. They sit back lazily on their haunches and make only the smallest motions, yet they never miss their aim. The inhabitant of Berne, who knows the pet name of each animal, is always amused by them, always watches them with a kind of pleased respect. He remembers that they are descendants of the bears which a Swiss army captured from the Duke of Milan at the beginning of the sixteenth century, and led back on leashes over the Alps to Berne.

Here we are half way through the first day of our trip and we have seen in a single morning Basel, a university city of the Rhenish type, the eastern plateau of the Jura, Neuchâtel and its lake painted with southern shadows, the opulent Bernese countryside and finally the Federal City, built on the crest and slopes of a long hill, and surrounded by a deep loop of the Aar. Three cities, three miniature worlds, more unlike than Boston and San Francisco, yet only one or two hours apart by railroad.

Now we penetrate further into Germanic (the Swiss avoid saying "German" since this war) Switzerland. Again the character of the dwellings changes. The farmhouses here are several stories high, with sharp-pointed roofs and white-barred windows which stand out against the blackened woodwork that covers a part of the façade. The men, too, have changed; they are smaller and darker, with red faces and awkward bodies. The orchards that cover their valleys and hills bear apples from which the peasants make a very sour cider with a high alcoholic content and the abuse of it for generations has injured the race. But cider is a tradition, and though the doctors advise against it the conservative clergy encourage the practice.

Here is the rain, for we are nearing Lucerne and the Lake of the Four Cantons, where the sky is gray 250 days a year. The hills now grow into mountains whose rocky bases are visible below the heavy clouds which hide the summits of the pre-Alps.

The Lake of Lucerne is a five-armed fiord, enclosed among the outposts of the Gothard Range. Its shores are so rich in historic memories that we might think ourselves in an open-air museum. Opposite Lucerne is Triebschen, Wagner's island, where Nietzsche loved Cosima without ever daring to admit it. On the nearby shore a monument recalls the death of the young Queen Astrid of Belgium. Further on is the villa of William II. Then we enter the region of the "holy places" of the Confederacy; the battlefield of Sempach, the Chapel built on the spot where legend says that William Tell leaped ashore to escape from the boat of the bailiff Gessler, and the hollow road where he waited to kill Gessler with an arrow from his crossbow. Opposite, on the southern bank, is a wooded hill with a meadow on top—the Rütli. There the first confederates representing the three primitive cantons swore the pact of 1291, and at midnight lit a beacon fire to give the signal of revolt against the Austrian overlords. This is the cradle of the idea of liberty which was later to take the name of democracy.

The longest arm of the Lake stretches north between rocky walls which grow higher and higher. In a chaos of leaden mist and blue-black depths the bastion of the Gothard is hidden. Night is coming on. We will spend it in Lucerne, a city of nineteenth century hotels in a medieval setting. On the morning of the second day, we turn southwest towards the Bernese Alps through the valley of the Unterwalden, which recalls with its bare, pointed hills and its sharp-toothed crags the landscapes of the German primitive painters. Passing in front of the gorge of the Ranft, where for twenty years the hermit Nicholas of Flue wielded over the Swiss a sort of spiritual dominion, we near another barren pass. On the far side of the tunnel we find ourselves in the heart of tourist Switzerland, above the lakes of Brienne and Thun, in a landscape so well known that it baffles description. The three great Alpine summits, the Jungfrau, Eiger, and Mönsch, which fill the background of the picture, have been so often portrayed that one comes to fancy that some painter of genius must have "composed" their powerfully balanced heights.

Brilliant, brand-new, pure, fresh—one would have

to repeat these adjectives about each element of the vast spectacle; the blue sky, the vaporous lakes, the grassy-green slopes, the white houses on the shores, the bright brown chalets grouped on the high plateau above the forest zone at the very foot of the crags, the domes of the translucid glaciers, and *névés* in the heights of the golden sky.

From Spez by the lakeside we rise slowly towards the Lötchberg, skirting the bottom of a valley through which runs a foaming stream whose gray waters roll along boulders and gleaming quartz. The slopes grow barer, the air fresher, the sky widens. At each little station, bright with travel posters and geraniums, the train deposits a troup of climbers who mingle with the peasants and the guides and porters of the hotels. Groups of people are singing on the platform to welcome friends or bid us good-by. There is a lyrical quality to this trip, born of the intense purity of the altitude, and the new lightness which it gives to all things here. We climb incessantly, passing by long winding curves and turning tunnels from one side of the valley to the other. One last spiral, and we stop in a circle of rocks and cascades. A little city of hotels surrounded by green meadows lies at the head of it, dominated perpendicularly by the blue slab of the glacier, which rises far above the rocks like a huge aquamarine. Here the railroad line disappears into a tunnel, a minute vaulted orifice at the foot of an enormous vertical wall of water-streaked granite, whose overhanging crests we can see by leaning out of the window.

Twenty minutes of noise in the night. We are going through the Lötchberg, under 6,000 feet of rock and snow. At the end of the tunnel the train stops in front of a long platform protected against avalanches by a cement arcade. The valley is narrow and desertic. Not a trace of green. A few ruined houses by the banks of a dried-up water-course. What sky can be seen between the rocks seems much lighter than on the other slope. We begin to go down southward. Deep ravines open out below the tracks; we cross from precipice to precipice on open bridges. Then come the first chestnut trees, a few with strangely distorted trunks. Suddenly, by a wide loop, we come out a thousand yards above the valley of the Rhône, a majestic gulf of lights and shadows where gray, olive-green, and red are the dominant tones. The river is a metallic yellow ribbon between embankments lined with rows of poplars, running through a plain cut by sand banks, by vineyards, and by forests, with here and there an old ruined tower. To the west where the vista is lost in mist a city rises upon the flanks of two rocks, crowned the one by a crenelated dungeon, the other by a church. It is Sion. To the north and south the slopes ascend broadly and regularly, covered at first with chestnut trees, then with meadows. Higher still appears the bare earth, reddish with purple-blue shadows, and behind the first line of crests a few white summits show against the violet clouds. Villages straggle along at different levels, and above timber-line blackened chalets cluster around a large white church. It is a vast landscape, simple in line, but one which the eye never wearies of scanning, finding everywhere—even in the desert heights—traces of the life of man.

The Valais constitutes a little world of its own. In the alluvial plain made by the Rhône grow southern crops, apricots and grapes on trellises. Above the forests begin the pasture lands and the Nordic vegetation. This is the level of the big villages, where all the peasants wear their black and white embroidered costumes. Higher up, those scattered chalets upon the crests are the alpages, stables and barns where the short perfumed summer hay is stored. Here the whole population moves according to the season from the level of the vineyards to the winter homes, then up into the summer pastures, ever struggling with a nature violent and full of contrasts, ever attuned to its rhythms.

While the train slowly crawls diagonally along the north slope of the main valley let us look down towards Brigue, at a high spur of rock topped by a little church and a cemetery. It is Rarogne. Seen from above, the village melts into the rocks which surround it, the pale pink Roman tiles scarcely distinguishable from the fallen granite shale. It is in this lovely cemetery near the old Lords of Rarogne that

Rilke chose to be buried. No one understood the Valais better than the poet who spent the last six years of his life a few miles away in a keep built in the twelfth century, the little castle of Muzot; a tower, a wide portal, a garden of roses and an orchard. No one saw more intensely this grandiose and violent landscape, nor perceived so clearly that it is an Alpine Spain.

Soon after the station of Brigue, which is swept by a hot wind laden with dust and particles of silex, we re-enter the flanks of the mountain. This is the tunnel of the Simplon which crosses the second Alpine chain. Another half hour of darkness—the Simplon is twenty-one miles long—and we come out into Italy. The mountains fall away rapidly, the first palm trees appear around the station. In a few moments, we glimpse the Lombard plain and Lake Maggiore, with the Isola Bella and its baroque gardens overladen with statues—one of the spots in the world most filled with literary associations and the memory of famous passions.

We have crossed Switzerland only in its narrowest dimension. We have seen neither Lake Leman nor Geneva to the west, nor the industrial region of Winterthur, nor Zurich, a modern and dynamic city, nor the orchards and banks of the Lake of Constance, nor the high valleys of the Engadine. Yet the contrasted sights have been rich enough to give us an idea of Switzerland "one yet diverse," according to the classic expression.

The impression which we have constantly had during this trip has been that at each stop we were in the midst of Europe, whether at Basel between France and Germany, at Neuchâtel between north and south, at Berne where all styles mingle harmoniously, or on the Simplon or the Lötchberg where the signs on the express train read suggestively: "Calais, Berne, Brindisi," or "Amsterdam, Zurich, Milan, Belgrade, Constantinople."

Switzerland has been called the turntable of Europe, but there is a still more vivid symbol of the central position of this country. In a little village at the foot of the Jura, there is a mill called the "Middle of the World" because from its large mill pond two streams flow, the one into the Aar and the Rhine, the other into Lake Geneva and the Rhône. It is the separation of the waters. When Germany declared war in 1914 the excellent but simple-minded miller closed the sluice gate which led to the Rhine, saying: "They shan't have any water in Germany!"

This is revealing of the Swiss character and attitude. Everywhere in this land men feel that they are in the middle of the world, never that they are in a remote corner. The Frenchman who does not live in Paris will dub himself provincial of his own accord; he feels that he is living apart from the currents of European civilization physically and spiritually. The

Swiss, even the countryman who only sees the international express train pass by his door every day nonetheless is never far from a linguistic or political frontier, and does not forget the existence of Europe and of other nearby peoples. That is perhaps why he travels and expatriates himself so willingly, in spite of his deep love for the spot of land where he spent his youth.

Each city, each village in Switzerland, has kept its personality, the product of its history and geography. The Swiss towns are wedded to their natural locations, whether these be the shore of a lake where the city spreads itself lengthwise, or the point of one which it embraces in its arms, or the slope of a hill which it climbs towards the cathedral and the castle, or a natural circle, as in Geneva, where the town has been organized about a central hill. In America, if you wake up in an hotel and look out the window you will seldom be able to guess where you are; nature has been suppressed, razed to the ground, and covered by buildings which are everywhere alike. In Switzerland you are enlightened at the first glance by a strip of lake, by the nearby or far-off Alps, by the Germanic or Latin aspects of façades and roofs, by the flowers, by the very window signs. You are located, yet at the same time you feel more than elsewhere that you are on one of the axes of Europe, at the center of a series of equally tempting lines of communication. When Paderewski was asked why he chose the little town of Morges on the shores of Lake Leman for his residence, he answered that above all it was because there he felt at an equal distance from all the great capitals where he gave his concerts.

A second trait which is common to all the regions of Switzerland is this mixture, this coexistence of all the periods of history with the most daring modernism. From the windows of our train we saw roads not as wide but quite as well built as American super-highways, running through old wooden-roofed bridges, painted and carved. We saw cities like Berne where one can move out from the medieval and renaissance center through districts built in the eighteenth and nineteenth centuries into suburbs which are astonishingly like the most ultra-modern cottage cities of America or Holland, grouped about clean up-to-date factories of the Le Corbusier style.

Finally, a scrutiny of the country from the geographical point of view leads us to a third fundamental fact. Through the defiles, the tunnels, the thresholds of valleys which brought so many changes of scene, we have passed from one compartment into another, from one milieu into a different one, from one community of customs and language into another very unlike.

A Swiss contemporary writer, Gonzague de Reynold, has admirably expressed the human importance of this physical fact. "If we try to gather from the land itself the natural laws which presided at the formation of the Swiss people, if we turn to the map we will note that the profile of the earth itself makes all this little country like a beehive. Whether on the plateau . . . or in the Jura or in the Alps . . . there are breaks, hollows, swellings, valleys and dales, compartments predestined each to have its own small community, just as each cell has its bee and its drop of honey.

"The Swiss land will thus impose on the people who come to build their homes in it a special political and social structure, the federal structure; a special constitutional principle, federalism."

Napoleon summed up this idea with one of his lapidary formulas in a speech made on December 12, 1802, to the Swiss Delegates in Paris: "Nature," he said, "has made your State federal. To try to overcome her is not the part of wisdom."

We will see how Swiss history has in the course of centuries fulfilled the destiny which nature itself prepared, and how upon the foundation of these very natural necessities the Swiss were able to erect their civic liberties.

III. A HISTORY OF LIBERTY

SWITZERLAND was born on that first day of August, 1291, of an Alliance of the "communes" of Uri, Schwytz, and Unterwalden, sworn by their representatives on the meadow of the Rütli. The alliance was recorded in a pact, nobly simple in language, whose importance is equaled only by Magna Carta and by the Declaration of the Rights of Man. But in contrast with the charter of the French Revolution we might call the Pact of 1291 a declaration of the duties of the citizen of a free Federation.

Here are its first and last clauses:

"In the Name of God, Amen. WE, the people of Uri, Schwyz, and Unterwalden, considering the evil times that are upon us and the better to protect and defend ourselves, swear upon oath to aid and succor one another mutually with our deeds and counsel, with our strong right arm and earthly goods, with all our might and soul, against each and all who do us hurt and wrong. With one voice do we swear and promise not to tolerate in our valleys the dominion of foreign overlords. None of us shall do harm unto a comrade whether to his body or to his possessions. He amongst us who shall be judged blameworthy shall repair his wrongdoing. Should discord arise between Confederates then shall our elders foregather and act as mediators. This our Covenant is drawn up for the good of all and shall, with God's help, endure for ever. Delivered in the year of Our Lord one thousand two hundred and ninety one in the beginning of the month of August."

"Shall, with God's help, endure forever." This clause has been vital to the development of the Confederation. It is always quoted in Swiss speeches, school books, and political meetings, for it is the one which contains the oath of fidelity. A federation, as the etymology of the word *foedus* indicates, is precisely a sworn alliance, a reciprocal engagement entered into by equals on the faith of an oath. It is the opposite of a power established by force, the imperial power of a man or a group. The Swiss State stands or falls by the unquestioned faith of the Pact, which has no assigned limits. That is why this Pact of 1291 is still the solemnly revered basis of the Confederation. Even today in many Swiss homes and schoolrooms, pictures which are products of the popular imagination represent the three founders of the Confederation, with their left hands joined and their right hands raised to Heaven. Switzerland was born of that gesture.

Yet we must beware of over-simplification, which is the fault of text-books. The oath of the three Swiss must be seen in its historic context. This does not detract from the greatness of the deed, but it does explain the conditions and the conflict of interests which made the Confederation possible.

In thirteenth-century Europe the Holy Roman Empire of the German nation loomed large. It was a vast construction which bound loosely together semi-sovereign states of various kinds: kingdoms, duchies, bishoprics, knight holdings, and free cities. It comprised roughly during that century the greater part of the German-speaking territories of Europe, and also a large part of Italy. But it was undergoing a serious crisis. Torn by the strife of the Guelfs and the Ghibellines (partisans of the Pope and the Emperor) it was threatened on the one hand by the growth of the liberal movement in the communes of northern Italy, Flanders and France, and on the other by the ambitions of powerful feudal houses, which were practicing a kind of reactionary "real-politik" and becoming more and more oppressive to their free subjects. One of the most illustrious of these was the House of Habsburg, whose strongholds were growing in number to the north of the present Switzerland, and whose lands were constantly extending in the region of the Gothard.

The forest Cantons of Uri and Schwytz dreaded the grasp of the Habsburgs. Since the latter were for the moment of the Pope's party, the "Waldstätten" naturally sought the help of the Emperor. Frederic II saw that it was to his interest to support them. The pass over the Gothard had been opened in the twelfth century, and the road passed first through the Valley of Uri, then through the territory of Schwytz. It was vital to the Emperor that this pass should not fall into Habsburg hands. Therefore his son and Vicar, Henri, granted the Imperial immediacy—that is to say, direct dependence on the Empire and freedom from feudal overlords—to Uri in 1231, and to Schwytz in about 1240.

These communities, long accustomed to govern themselves, and to organize cooperatives (*Markgenossenschaften*) for the exploitation of the forests, as the nature of their land required, thus became small rural free states, analogous to the Imperial cities.

As the reactionary policies of the overlords became more marked, the Forest Cantons grew more consciously resolute to be free. The merchants, clerics and muleteers who crossed the Gothard kept the free men of Uri and Schwytz informed as to all that was going on across the Alps, and taught them to contract alliances on the strength of an oath, on the model of the urban communes of Lombardy. The latest of these was the Pact of 1291. It was the *only* one among hundreds of analogous alliances concluded in Italy and elsewhere which managed to endure through the centuries and become the basis of a genuine State.

This unique success can be explained by a combination of very complex circumstances. The geographical fact of the Gothard, the social fact of the existence of Markgenossenschaften, the political fact of the struggle of the Habsburgs with the Emperor are the three principal factors which helped to crystallize and to maintain the communal tendency in that precise spot in Europe. In Italy, the communes degenerated into tyrannies, Germany turned more and more towards a "real-politik," and France was centralized under the influence of its Kings. "The Forest Cantons alone kept the inheritance of the civic liberties of the Middle Ages, and successfully resisted the general evolution of the age towards monarchy. By a tenacious struggle they not only won the democratic right of self-determination, but at last founded the League of the Swiss States. The birth of the Confederation and its successful defense are, then, unique in the annals of the late Middle Ages, and the history of the peasants of western Europe contains few facts as surprising. The problem of Swiss scientific historians will always be that of making this event intelligible. Of the struggle for the democratic and communal idea which took place in that era the Swiss Confederation is the only surviving institution. It represents the result of a general revolution which was elsewhere defeated. Of all the battles waged for liberty by the peasants of western Europe that one alone resulted in a lasting creation, a creation which was later enriched by the addition of urban elements." [1] It is the growth of this first federal nucleus which we must now examine.

The story of William Tell is too familiar to be retold here—after Schiller and some hundred of other chroniclers and dramatists. The historical existence of that hero of the cross-bow has never been satisfactorily established. Moreover, eloquent though the myth of Tell may be, no individual hero should be allowed to obscure the collective reality of the origins of the Confederation, especially since this less-known reality is highly significant for our own times. To know the true story of these beginnings may warn us against the illusions which abound today among creators of systematic and rationalized plans for the federation of peoples.

The makers of the Pact whence Switzerland was born did not decide to found a new State nor create a new form of government. They united to remain free and to be ready to accomplish the task that the Emperor had given them. It was realistically—driven always by the physical conditions of their country—that they gradually widened their Alliance, which reached the final figure of twenty-two cantons only in 1815, that is to say, after five centuries. Uri, Schwytz and Unterwalden first saw the need of incorporating

[1] Ernest Gagliardi: *Histoire de la Suisse.*

in their Alliance the city of Lucerne, which commanded the approaches of the Gothard, and which had an armed force that was respected by the neighboring feudal lords. Thus a first nucleus of four cantons was formed. This group soon allied itself with the Imperial city of Zurich, then conquered with the help of that city the cantons of Glaris and Zoug and, proceeding to give these valleys their autonomy, it made them allies on a basis of equality. Next they made a pact with the city of Berne, which already had an alliance with Zurich, and was soon to conquer and make into subject provinces the land of Vaud and the Argovian plateau.

Thus to the first League of the Forest Cantons were added during the fourteenth and fifteenth centuries three allied groups whose centers were respectively in Appenzell to the north, in Berne to the west, and in the Grisons to the northeast. By the beginning of the sixteenth century the Confederation comprised thirteen sovereign cantons.

It would require many pages merely to enumerate the complicated series of alliances which bound these cantons together. What should particularly be noted is that several cantons belonged to two groups of allies, and that the alliances were not always entirely reciprocal in their obligations. It was as though today two countries should sign a treaty which obliged one contracting party to give active assistance, while the other merely pledged non-aggression. For our purposes what stands out from the history of those centuries is the pluralistic character of Swiss federalism. It gave to each city or valley its own special role within the general Alliance, and respected the local interests and the particular needs of each. Thus, it favored the freedom of every member of the League, without lessening the needed cohesion of the whole in times of war. It was, in fact, the Swiss cantons which first evolved and practiced, in a way that has never been equaled since, the policy of mutual assistance and collective security.

"The principal and first chapter of all the Alliances and Leagues," wrote a sixteenth-century chronicler, Josias Simler, "concerns the help which each must give the others against those who would unjustly attack them. When once the injustice has been established the canton involved can call on all the Confederates to succor it . . . each canton is not allied with every other, yet though we have not all the same rights nonetheless if one canton asks two or more allies to come to its help all the cantons assemble—the first called having notified the others."

What strikes us most today in the history of the old Confederation is the strength of the communal spirit. It was that spirit alone which enabled so informal a political system to function. We have already pointed out that the very nature of the land forced the peasants of the central region to work in groups and render each other mutual aid. The political mission which was entrusted to them in exchange for their liberties merely accentuated their need for solidarity; they had to unite for protection against those without. But within the Federation the communal spirit manifested itself in two characteristic ways: in a struggle against any hegemony within the League and in a mistrust of "great men."

The idea is abroad today that a federation can only be formed under the aegis of some organizing power. The example of the British Commonwealth of Nations is often quoted in support of this thesis, but that of the Swiss Confederation seems to refute the contention. The Swiss Federation was founded and consolidated precisely through a constant struggle against all efforts at hegemony, whether the attempt came from a city richer than the country districts or from a group of cantons having common interests. Thus the primitive cantons made war on Zurich when that city attempted to take the leadership of the League.

Every time one of the cantons thought that the time had come to impress its own particular policies upon the Federation, it found all the other members spontaneously leagued against it, and each time the final result was a tightening of the Alliance on a basis of real equality, the smaller cantons receiving legal advantages to balance the material advantages of the larger ones.

In the social field this instinctive rejection of all hegemony took from the first the form of a peculiar kind of equalitarianism, which deeply affected and still affects Swiss customs and habits. At that time it was not in the least a question of establishing an abstract equality of citizens before the law, such as was created by the French Revolution. Most Swiss peasants were already "free men," but the feudal seigneur remained lord of his land, and several cantons possessed bailiwicks which were really subject states, and which they sometimes harshly oppressed. The equalitarianism of the early Swiss showed itself as an active mistrust of over-advertised personalities, of men who did not sufficiently hide their superiority, or who, taking on the appearance of a *Führer,* threatened to draw the country into adventures.

This mistrust was the negative side of the vague yet widespread consciousness of a mission which precluded imperialistic or dictatorial aims. The few who did not efface themselves in time, such as the reformer, Zwingli, or the statesman of Zurich, Waldemann, came to an ill end, the former killed in battle, the latter murdered.

This instinctive reaction of the federated citizens was in a measure wholesome and authentically democratic. It is the kindest explanation of certain unpleasant traits of the modern Swiss character. Inevitably in the course of the centuries, as the sense of a mission lessened, an equalitarianism once vital degenerated little by little into a taste for the mediocre, and an ill will towards those who are "too outstanding" into a desire to reduce all to the level of the average. This has often driven the most creative as well as the most turbulent of her sons to leave Switzerland and expatriate themselves, in order to escape from the dumb, half-conscious persecution of public opinion.

To return to facts, from the twelfth to the thirteenth century the history of Switzerland is that of a long struggle between the cantons and the Habsburgs. As that dynasty gradually strengthened its hold on the Empire and established an hereditary right to the Imperial crown, it lost ground in its land of origin. A series of Swiss victories, each more astonishing than the other, mark this period.

For instance, at the battle of Morgarten 600 Swiss exterminated a "Panzerdivision" of 11,000 heavily armed knights. It has been recently discovered that the army of the Habsburgs was composed of feudal lords from all countries in Europe. The adherence of these feudal lords to the Habsburg cause can be explained by rumors then current as to the republican and antifeudal organization of the Swiss communes, and their violent desire for independence, which had made the name Swiss almost synonymous with the spirit of revolution. The word "Schwyzer" was used at that time much as we loosely use the terms "bolshevik" or "anarchist" today. Maximilian of Austria called any of his rebellious subjects, whether Croatian or Bohemian, "Swiss."

Later at the battle of Sempach, victory was won for the cantons by one man, Arnold of Winkelried, who threw himself upon the Austrian lances, and gathering them into his own breast, opened a breach in the square.[2] But the battle which added most to the Swiss reputation as fighting men was that of St. Jacques sur la Birse, in 1444. Desperately inferior in numbers, the Swiss knew that all they could do was to fight to the death. This they did, and they were killed to the last man; but they inflicted such losses on the French that the latter had to retire. On the evening of the battle, Louis, riding over the battlefield and seeing the corpses, exclaimed, "I am walking in a field of roses." "Smell this one, too!" cried a mortally wounded Swiss, throwing a stone red with his blood at the Duke's head.

The battle of St. Jacques sur la Birse is an example of defense at all costs which the political and moral authorities of Switzerland have put forward during the present war. It illustrates the motto of the oath in Schiller's *Tell:* "Better death than slavery." The troops mobilized in 1939 have often been reminded of it.

Following the Burgundian wars, during which the Swiss defeated and killed Charles the Bold, the rich-

[2] Legend has it that as he rushed forward Winkelried cried: "Confederates, I will open you a path. Take care of my wife and children." But the Swiss, ever mistrustful of theatrical gestures, have it that he said as he fell, "Who is the pig who pushed me?" This national joke is very popular.

est and strongest prince of his time, whom neither the Austrians nor the French had been able to master, the little Confederation became the first military power in Europe. The Swiss crossed the Alps, invaded Lombardy, took Milan, and annexed the county of Bellinzona, that is to say the whole southern slope of the Gothard. They crossed the Rhine, invaded Swabia, and beat the armies of the Emperor. Eastern France, Italy, Southern Germany were open to their conquest. Would the guardians of the pass betray their Imperial mission and become empire builders on their own account?

The half century which passed between the Burgundian wars and the Reformation was decisive for the destiny of the Confederation, to which it brought both its severest test and its greatest glory. Certain mighty personalities stand out in this period, those of Nicholas of Flue, of Cardinal Schinner, and of Zwingli. These three characters symbolize each of the three acts of the drama in which the destiny of the Confederation was played out.

Nicholas was born at a time when the Council of Constance was laboring to restore the unity of the Church after the great schisms. He came of a family of free and rich peasants of the Unterwalden. Even in childhood he performed the duties of religion with an almost eccentric scrupulousness. He ate nothing on Fridays and often fasted on other days. His piety seemed to destine him for holy orders, but when he came to manhood he entered one of the armed bands which were fighting against Austria, and became Roltmeister, a sort of captain. Disgusted by the futile brutality of the expeditions in which he took part, he retired to his native canton, and became a Justice of the Peace there. One day a flagrant injustice caused him to resign his office. This sort of withdrawal was the pattern of his life.

Yet this captain, this judge, this father—he had ten children—was a kind of man not unusual in the Confederation of that day. He was a solid and sensible citizen, although his intimates felt the long drama of his inner struggle.

Doubtless he had visions, and perhaps he dreamt, as did his century, of a more direct contact with God. At fifty he could no longer resist. His vocation overcame all his doubts and his human bonds. He told his wife of his decision, and she accepted it at the price of an heroic struggle with herself.

Then began the solitude and prayer which he had longed for as the culmination of a life's evolution. He built a cell and a tiny chapel in the gorges of the Ranft, only an hour from his home. The miracle of his childhood came true—he could do without food! Once a week he went to communion in a nearby village—that was all he ate. Neither the spies set about his cell by the authorities, nor the emissaries of the Bishop ever caught him at fault. The legend of his piety grew, and pilgrims came in numbers to the

Ranft. Princes sent envoys to consult him, for his advice became all-powerful with the Swiss. Thus he advised them to be prudent in regard to the Duke of Burgundy, for he saw the dangers into which victory would plunge them. If they made war to grow rich they would learn the price of gold, and their patriarchal union would be lost.

But the temptation was too strong. The Swiss neglected the hermit's advice, and all his prophecies came true. Victory brought quarrels over the division of spoils. Things went so ill that by 1486 fifteen Diets had not succeeded in re-establishing the union. At last a Diet met at Stans. Agreements seemed impossible, and the delegates separated with threats of civil war. This was Nicholas' hour. During the night the priest of Stans climbed to the Ranft and begged the hermit to make a last effort. No one knows what message Nicholas gave him. What the formal documents testify is that at dawn the priest, returning to Stans, called the delegates together and in secret session gave them Nicholas' advice. Was it a miracle or the result of some political "combination" of which the hermit suggested the idea? Probably the influence of Nicholas was enough to quiet men's spirits, and allow them to make mutual concessions. At all events the Diet proclaimed that if peace and the fate of the Confederation had been saved, it was owing above all to the action of the hermit of the Ranft.

Nicholas represented the true Swiss tradition: realism, poverty, spiritual vision, fidelity to the primitive alliance. The mighty prince of the Church, Matthias Schinner, was in almost every point the exact opposite of the lay hermit. A son of Valaisan peasants, by force of shrewdness and will he slowly rose to the highest honors, to become a cardinal and a statesman more powerful than the Pope, and a great strategist into the bargain. Cardinal Schinner incarnated the imperialistic temptation against which Nicholas of Flue warned the free cantons. His dream was to consolidate in the midst of Europe a great State comprising Lombardy, Burgundy, and Swabia, and centered in the regions around the Gothard under the domination of the Swiss Confederacy. The military power of the Swiss at that time seemed to justify such an enterprise, but had it succeeded it would have meant the end of the Confederacy, for a powerful State centering in the Gothard would have been a perpetual menace to the neighboring nations which were in process of formation, and especially to France, which Schinner hated. Such a State, involved in all the European struggles for power, would have been obliged to become strong and unified, in order that annexed provinces should not acquire too much influence and civil war result in final dismemberment. Nothing could be more contrary to the federal spirit than such a strong unified power.

For two centuries the Confederation existed without a capital or a legal center, and with no written constitution save the pact of 1291. Its Diet, composed of delegates from the cantonal governments, met spontaneously as need arose in one city or another, and it had no clearly defined powers, although its authority was decisive in certain cases. It was this unsystematic system, habitual and customary, but not legalistic, based on the civic sense of the Confederates rather than on rigid texts—it was, in a word, the spirit of the Helvetian Confederation—which the ambitions symbolized by Cardinal Schinner were imperiling.

At first he was very successful in leading the Swiss troops into Italy on several lightning expeditions. The Duchy of Milan became virtually a protectorate of the Confederates. Thus they were in a measure arbiters of the fate of the peninsula for which the Emperor and the King of France were struggling. At Novara, in 1513, Louis XII was utterly defeated by them. But at Marignano, in 1515, the Swiss were obliged to abandon the field after two days of a struggle which was gigantic for that era. Their slow and solemn retreat—for, fighting step by step, they carried off all their dead and wounded—was the last great feat of the old Confederation. This bloody twilight of Marignano ended the heroic dream of Schinner, although the military reverse would not alone have sufficed to bring the Swiss back within their former limits. A phenomenon of a different order was about to constrain them from within—the Reformation.

Modern historians have sometimes accused Zwingli of breaking the military energy of the Confederation, its drive towards the sea, and towards adventure. In our opinion Zwingli and his reforms saved Switzerland and returned it to its primitive destiny.

Zwingli had grown up in the disorder of the period of war, of general corruption, and of feverish ambitions. He had witnessed the results of these practices close at hand, as almoner in the wars of Italy. He was a great humanist, realistic by nature, more of a rationalist than a mystic, a born statesman. All these are characteristics which distinguish him from Luther.

He was first noted for his violent diatribes against the system of mercenaries and the foreign alliances. He liked to quote the warnings of Nicholas of Flue, and he brought the political ideal of the hermit to realization.

He had been abbot of the famous monastery of Einsiedeln, which was a center of humanistic culture. But it was as a priest in Zurich that he began to introduce ecclesiastical reforms analogous to those of Luther. The whole population was behind him, and when the Emperor, uneasy at the growth of the Reformation, sought to attack Zurich with the help of the central cantons, which had remained Catholic, Zwingli was given charge of the defense of the city. His political power grew as his religious work took on wider scope. In his opinion Church and State could not be separated, and the régime which he imposed little by little on the cantons which adopted the Reformation deserves much more than that of Calvin the title of theocracy.

He defeated the Catholic cantons in a series of local wars, and after 1528 he became the most important religious and political leader not only of the Confederation but of all Southern Germany. Unfortunately Luther did not reach an understanding with him at the time of the famous Colloquy of Marburg in 1529, and this disagreement caused the failure of the grandiose plan which the Zurichois had conceived. This plan was a system of alliances among the German and Swiss cities, into which little by little France, Denmark and Venice would have been drawn. Zwingli believed that such a European Confederation would have been able to overthrow the Habsburgs who had taken possession of the Empire. But the Lutheran princes were cold to this idea. In Zurich itself there was a growing opposition to the Reformer. The Catholics had nicknamed him "the Bailiff of all the Confederates." Berne mistrusted his ambition. At last a Catholic army neared Zurich. The Protestants wanted to negotiate. Zwingli was for war. Half betrayed by his compatriots, he was beaten at Kappel, massacred on the battlefield, and his body drawn, quartered and burned the next day. As he donned his armor on the morning of the battle, he admitted to his wife that he felt the darkest forebodings. His tragic end brought to a close the Shakespearean drama of the Swiss Renaissance.

Weakened by its religious struggles, but assured of its independence by the victories which it had won over the French, the Imperialists, and the Italians, its territory increased in every direction—towards the Rhine, towards Burgundy and Lombardy—Switzerland was to enjoy a long period of peace and creative neutrality. At the congress of Münster in Westphalia in 1648, which ended the 30 Years' War, it obtained the recognition of this neutrality, and formally separated itself from the Empire. This was merely the recognition of a fact which had existed since the end of the fifteenth century. Germany was definitely orienting itself towards a policy of dynastic power, whereas Switzerland was keeping to the old ideal of its imperial liberties. Rather than a break with the Empire, it was, as historians have pointed out, "a refusal to incorporate itself in a denatured Empire"—an act of fidelity to its eternal mission as guardian of the heart of Europe.

The Reformation ended Switzerland's period of heroic adventure and expansion, but inaugurated one of spiritual growth. The Confederation was stabilized, it had won the respect of the Powers, and it withdrew into a kind of political isolation. What use would it make of the era of peace? The seventeenth and eighteenth centuries were to give Switzerland a long respite from foreign history. Few or no wars or territorial modifications, but a slow and minute work of social organization and cultural ripening were to take place.

As early as the beginning of the sixteenth century the cultural vocation of Switzerland had shown itself in the creation of centers of intellectual activity. Basel with Erasmus attracted the humanistic printers, Zurich with Zwingli was the starting point of the Swiss religious revolt, and Geneva under Calvin was the heart of the international Reformation.

The period between the Reformation and the French Revolution was for Switzerland one of systole, of a contraction of forces, and to some extent of political and social reaction. The central cantons continued to govern themselves by the system of the Landesgemeinde, that is to say, through the election of functionaries and the ratification of laws by vote of all the citizens assembled in a public place. But the cantons whose center was a city of some importance—Zurich, Lucerne, Soleure, Berne, Basel, as well as the allied cities of Neuchâtel and Geneva—became oligarchical republics. A certain number of noble or patrician families exercised in them a sort of hereditary power, because they alone or almost alone furnished the representatives in the Small Council, which beside or above the Grand Council of the three Estates made the laws and named the administrators. The burgesses kept their liberties and their share in the communal possessions, and they had a voice in the Grand Council, but practically the nobility controlled the destinies of these little cantonal republics.

It is in the nature of hereditary power to degenerate, with too much security, into an ever greater mediocrity. Goethe, traveling in Switzerland at the end of the eighteenth century, wrote in his diary:

"Once the Swiss rid themselves of a tyrant. They thought for a time that they were free, but the fecund sun bred from the corpse of the oppressor a swarm of petty tyrants. Today they repeat to satiety that they freed themselves and have remained free. In reality behind their walls they are slaves, though only to their laws, their customs, and their bourgeois prejudices."

In the small republics of Italy at the beginning of the nineteenth century there was a certain stuffiness of atmosphere, a narrowness of life and outlook. It seems probable that the same limitations, what the French call the odor of the shut-in, existed in the Swiss communities, and that this offended Goethe. His criticism, however, seems exaggerated. Rousseau, who had tasted in France of a tyranny more real than gossip, took refuge in Berne, the most strictly aristocratic of all the cantons, and on crossing the frontier he got out of his carriage and throwing himself on the ground, kissed it, saying: "I greet the soil of liberty!" There is a curious comparison to be made between

Rousseau and the socialists and revolutionaries who today seek refuge in the United States, land of capitalistic oligarchy. In comparison with the Europe of absolute monarchies, of the *corvée,* the *gabelle* and the *lettres de cachet,* aristocratic and republican Switzerland had kept a certain spirit of liberty whose importance could be measured at the time of the French Revolution.

We have spoken of political contraction in Switzerland during the seventeenth and eighteenth centuries. There was, however, a curious phenomenon, one unexampled in other countries, which acted during this period as a sort of compensation for that contraction—this was foreign military service. The Swiss have often been accused of lacking the spirit of adventure, and it is true that the exiguity of their lands and resources has forbidden them to indulge in much violence of action or imagination, but it should not be forgotten that Switzerland of all countries in the world has exported the largest number of hot-heads. The Confederation was neutral, but the fighting blood of its sons was not as readily cooled as the mind of its politicians. The Diet met the difficulty by allowing officers to raise regiments on their own account and to offer their services to foreign princes. These men were not mercenaries in the technical sense. The nobles who possessed regiments did not rent them to a foreign government, but allied themselves to that government according to a treaty system known as that of Capitulations. Often they formed the royal bodyguard. Thus Pfyffer's regiment saved the life of Charles IX during the retreat from Meaux in 1567, and as a result of this exploit the Pfyffers obtained the privilege of speaking with covered head to the King of France. In the same way the Swiss Guards were the last to protect Louis XVI against the mob on August 10, 1792, and were almost all massacred on the steps of the Tuileries.

The history of the Swiss in the foreign service is associated with that of the most brilliant battles of these centuries, many of which were won through their intervention. Soldiers of the cantons were to be found serving the Kings of France, of Prussia, of England, the States General of Holland, the Realm of Naples, the King of Spain and the Emperor of Austria. They were to be found in the Colonies—it was a regiment from Neuchâtel which took the City of Seringapatam for the British East India Company.

At a battle during the war of the Austrian Succession Swiss troops fought on both sides. The men of a regiment from Berne in the service of France recognized with horror blue and yellow uniforms like their own in the English ranks opposite them. They were the colors of the von May family and the colonels of the two regiments were cousins. As a result of this fratricidal battle the Diet decided that when there were Swiss on both sides they should not be obliged to fire.

It is to the period of foreign service that the well-known saying "No money, no Swiss!" refers. The saying is unjust, for it was not merely for money, which in case of defeat was not always paid, but for glory and because of their military tradition that tens of thousands of Swiss chose to expatriate themselves.

A French prince once said to a Swiss officer who wanted pay for his men, "With the money that we have already given you one could pave a road from Paris to Basel!" The officer replied, "With the blood my men have shed for France one could fill a canal from Basel to Paris." An old story familiar to all Swiss tells that a Frenchman once reproached a Swiss soldier because he fought for money. "And what do you fight for?" asked the other. "For honor!" said the Frenchman. "Oh, well, each fights for what he has not got," returned the Swiss.

It must be admitted that the 750 marshals and generals and the thousands of officers of lower rank that Switzerland gave to the armies of Europe did not all come back empty-handed. Many brought home gold and silver, rare plate, furniture, jewels, arms and other precious reminders of their foreign campaigns. Considerable treasures were thus amassed in Swiss châteaux from generation to generation. Many also brought back patents of nobility or wives who were the daughters of foreign nobles. Thus the Swiss aristocracy became one of the most international in Europe both by allegiance and by blood.

As for the common soldiers, once their engagement was ended they returned to the land or set up shop in the cities. They would tell their experiences under the linden tree of the public square, describing foreign lands and customs, and teach their children the songs of the regiment. A considerable folklore, rich in small masterpieces of charm, irony or melancholy, was born of the foreign service and has survived in country districts to this day.

The epic of the foreign service was to end in the memorable retreat from Russia, closing at the Beresina in 1813, just as the epic of primitive Switzerland closed three centuries earlier on the plains of Marignano. Decimated by cold and disease, harassed by the Cossacks, the Grand Army marched for weeks across the Russian steppes. The rear guard stopped beside the Beresina to allow the body of the troops to cross the last remaining bridge. As usual the Swiss were ordered to cover the retreat. They spent the night trying to keep warm beside the bivouac fires.

"The hours passed slowly. The snow, noiselessly falling, covered the companies, the squadrons, the batteries. Long before dawn Commander Blattmann and Lieutenant Legler wrapped in their great coats were walking to and fro along the road to Stakow to shake off the torpor of the night. The thought of death passed between them.

"Do you remember," said Blattmann, "that song that you used to like so much at Glaris?"

Legler began to hum softly.

"Our life is the journey of a pilgrim in the night.

"Each finds in his furrow his own pursuing grief."

His voice rose, warm and vibrant. A few officers drew near, and soldiers got up to listen to the song which penetrated them to the heart, waking in them the magic of memory. A group gathered, men came from all sides, drawn by the echo of their far-off native land. Hundreds of voices took up the couplets. The song grew, passing over the bivouacs and floating across the white plains.

"On with our journey,

"Brothers, march on to danger.

"After the night and storm

"Sunrise will come."

It was the reveille of the Swiss in the gray dawn, their farewell to life, their greeting to their country. The huge voice of the cannon had already begun to sing a muffled bass, and a burst of musketry fire crackled to the right. . . .

As the daylight brightened, the commanding officers of the regiment stood before the ranks.

"Soldiers, we have been given the post of honor; we must hold here while the whole army retreats behind us by the road to Zem. We know that you will maintain your old reputation. Today we must die for the glory of the Swiss name."

"The officers, gathered together before the men, shook hands and solemnly swore to each other 'to fight to the last man, not to look to the wounded, and to keep before their eyes the honor of Switzerland.' "[3]

The Swiss lost eighty per cent of their men, but they accomplished the task which had been entrusted to them. They lived up to the motto which was on every flag, "Honor and fidelity."

At home, in the meantime, the outbreak of the French Revolution found Switzerland with no unified army, no central power, given over to the intrigues of French agents who stirred the people against the oligarchies. The country was in no shape to resist the invasion of the revolutionary armies. Berne was pillaged and all the silver accumulated in its patrician houses was melted in the Cathedral Square to be made into French money. For several years the Helvetian Republic, "one and indivisible," highly centralized on the Jacobin model which the French imposed on the Swiss, was the theater of a struggle between the armies of the allies, Prussia, Austria, Russia, and those of the Convention and of Bonaparte. But the dumb yet obstinate resistance of the civilian population, the constant risings in the central valleys, at last won Napoleon's respect, and made him understand that it was useless to hope to subdue a people whose tradition of liberty was five centuries older than the Revolution. In a speech to the Swiss Delegates to Paris in 1802 he made large concessions to

[3] Pierre de Vallière: *Honneur et Fidélité.*

the cantons, and uttered a commendation of federalism astonishing in the hero of the Jacobins:

"Without the democracies of your little cantons you would have nothing which cannot be found elsewhere; you would have no particular color. Think how important it is to have characteristic traits; it is these traits which, by contradicting the idea of resemblance to other states, remove that of confounding you with them, of incorporating you in them." [4]

The treaties of 1814 and 1815, although they were based on opposition to nationalism, did not attempt to dismember Switzerland. On the contrary, they solemnly reasserted that the independence, the inviolability and neutrality of the Confederation were in the true interests of Europe. Swiss neutrality became an essential part of the new system. "The declaration of March 20, 1815," writes Guglielmo Ferrero, "is the door whereby Switzerland entered the great century of its history, the one in which it was to create the most human order that the world has seen." [5] This régime, a synthesis of the old liberty-loving yet conservative federalism and of certain principles of the Revolution, took thirty years to evolve.

The wars and upheavals of the Revolution and Empire left Switzerland uneasy. The oligarchical régimes had proved themselves unable to resist foreign

[4] Napoleon. Speech of December 12, 1802, to the Swiss Delegates in Paris.

[5] G. Ferrero: *Reconstruction.*

attack, and the need for some kind of central power was evident. New cantons, long bound to Switzerland, had now officially entered the Federal Alliance. They were Geneva, Vaud (at last free of the domination of Berne), Neuchâtel, Valais, and the Ticino. While the federation of thirteen cantons had been almost wholly Germanic, that of twenty-two now included French- and Italian-speaking regions important enough to demand equality. All the old problems were again to be solved on a larger scale. From 1815 to 1847 there was much political effervescence, sometimes breaking out in riots. Revolutionary ideas gained ground. The "radical" party demanded a single constitution and the extension and codification of popular rights.

The latent struggle became much more serious when in 1847 the Federal Diet decreed the expulsion of the Jesuits, and the Catholic cantons formed a separate League, the Sonderbund, to resist them. The army of the Protestant cantons, led by General Guillaume Henri Dufour, put down in a very brief campaign the forces of the Catholic cantons. "Soldiers," Dufour had said in his first proclamation to the troops, "we must come out of this war not only victorious but without reproach. Men must say of us that we fought when we had to but that we showed ourselves generous and humane." Dufour applied these same principles after the victory.

The war of the Sonderbund, which has often been

compared to the American War of Secession, resulted in a strengthening of the Federal Alliance. The Diet of 1848 was very generous to the vanquished. They were helped to pay their war debt by public subscription, raised for the most part in the Protestant cantons. In fact the contrast between the policies of Switzerland and of the United States after a civil war is striking. The result of the wisdom and tolerance of the Swiss was an atmosphere of internal harmony in which Switzerland was able peacefully to make its first written Constitution. After 500 years the League of the Cantons became a true Federal State with an army, a budget, and a centralized executive power—the Federal Council.

It was only after 1848 that Switzerland became a democracy in the technical meaning of the word, and the long tradition of civic responsibility and of vigorous autonomy which remained in its communes and its cantons, as well as its relative tardiness in assimilating certain of the revolutionary ideas, combined to give the new Confederation exceptional stability.

In 1874 the Constitution was easily adapted to the new necessities created by the economic development of the country. These obviously tended to bring about a growing centralization. Therefore until the present war the crux of all political discussions in Switzerland was the problem of the respective rights of the cantons and the Confederation.

The peaceful era of 1848 to 1914 allowed Switzerland to devote herself increasingly to her international mission. A mere citizen, Henry Dunant, founded the International Red Cross; the Federal Council devoted large sums of money to building the tunnels of the St. Gothard, the Lötchberg and the Simplon, by which the neighboring nations were to profit even more than Switzerland; and other international institutions chose to fix their central seat in Switzerland. Thus the original function of the country found its modern expression, one that was to reveal itself strikingly during the war of 1914 to 1918.

After a century of growing nationalism, the first world war, which set the German and Latin worlds at odds, was for Switzerland a crucial test of its Federalism. Would not the French and Italian cantons take sides with the Allies and the German cantons with the Central Powers? This did happen in a sense. For four years a moral gulf existed between the two linguistic groups. It seemed a miracle to outsiders that political passions did not break up the Confederation. In reality they divided the country scarcely more than an electoral campaign divides the United States.

For four years in spite of often violent divergencies in sympathy on the part of the High Command, the Swiss Army faithfully watched at the frontiers. Moreover the frequent shifting of French Swiss troops into Germanic territories and vice versa tended to strengthen rather than to weaken the adherence of all Swiss to their common "nation," that is to say to a super-national, super-racial, super-linguistic ideal.

As in the days of the Reformation, of monarchical absolutism, and of the French Revolution, Switzerland again became the land of refuge for the exiled and the persecuted of all countries. Sienkiewicz, Romain Rolland, Lenin found refuge there. But above all, Switzerland became a sort of vast international ambulance. Tens of thousands of prisoners, sick or severely wounded, from both camps were there received and nursed in the summer and winter resorts, now empty of tourists. Hotel of Europe in peacetime, Switzerland became its hospital during the war.

Because of its neutrality and its central position, it was the spot where most of the secret conversations between belligerents took place. It was also, less happily, a center of international espionage. In the castles and homes of the Swiss aristocracy, often related to both sides, unofficial emissaries could meet as it were by accident. In 1917, in a house in Neuchâtel, Prince Sixte de Bourbon Parme tried to negotiate a separate peace for Austria, which was almost realized. At the same time in the cafés of Zurich and Geneva, Lenin was meeting German agents and preparing the famous trip in a sealed railway carriage which was to take him, with the consent of the Kaiser's government, to Finland.

In warring countries people snatched at the Swiss newspapers, the only ones which gave both the French and the German communiqués, as well as more or less impartial judgments on events. More or less . . . for sympathy for the Allies or for Germany was evident in the editorials of the Swiss press. In 1917, when peace rumors were abroad, the Germans used to say: "The Allies would like to make peace, but the *Gazette de Lausanne* won't let them." Yet on the whole Swiss opinion was remarkably objective and cool.

In the period between the two wars it seemed that Switzerland was to have an opportunity to crown its century-old mission. The League of Nations in deciding to fix its abode in Geneva paid a striking tribute to the super-national part the Confederation had played since the far-off days of the Holy Roman Empire. It seemed that the history of this little country was to find its culmination in the development of a World Federation with its capital in Switzerland.

But once the first enthusiasm was over, the prudent Swiss, who are experts in federalism, saw the weaknesses of an organism which was too theoretically and too hastily constructed, too ill-rooted in the conscience of peoples to offer much guarantee of permanence.

Cautiously, because of its faith in the continuity of its own history, which it did not think was ended, the Swiss Confederation asked for and obtained a special status in the League. It is partly to this prudence, which many considered exaggerated at the time, that Switzerland owes the fact that it has so far been spared in the second world war. Had the country been too closely involved with a League which might by the force of circumstances have become an instrument of British policy, it would perhaps have paid dearly for this deviation from its traditional attitude.

Today Switzerland is reduced to its simplest expression, to its original peril and greatness. Two physical images illustrate both the real position and the significant destiny of the country. In Geneva the Palace of the Nations, finished shortly before the outbreak of war, is empty, and guarded by anti-aircraft guns and soldiers with loaded rifles. On the other hand, around the powerfully fortified Gothard, age-old center of Swiss life, the nine divisions of the Swiss Army, one of the best trained in the world, mount guard day and night, ready to blow up the tunnel and the road, ready to resist the invader with all the resolution of a people which has always known what it has to defend.

A sentence of Alexander Vinet, the nineteenth century Swiss philosopher and theologian, seems to sum up the essential meaning of the history which we have here briefly recalled. This maxim was written in monumental letters on the walls of the central pavilion of the National Exhibition of 1939 in Zurich, and every Swiss citizen who read it understood its concrete historical meaning, both collective and individualistic.

"I want man to be master of himself that he may the better be the servant of all."

IV. A MULTIPLE STATE

JACOB BURCKHARDT said of the Swiss that their State is their masterpiece. In the same vein, Lord Bryce in his book on modern democracies put Switzerland first of all the countries that he studied in the qualities which he considered as criteria of a well-functioning democracy. These are: the intelligence of the average man, the extent to which the educated classes interest themselves in public affairs, and the existence of a sense of national unity and an active public opinion. It is significant that these criteria are social, not political, and Lord Bryce recognized that it is, in fact, the temper of the people quite as much as their constitution which makes any form of government successful.

Until 1848 the Confederation was not a nation—scarcely even a State in the technical sense. It was rather a League of Sovereign States, a kind of miniature League of Nations. Its Diet was not a government but a council of ambassadors, who acted under mandate from the cantonal Governments and had no clear legislative nor executive powers.

Two principal factors induced the cantons of the

Confederation to enter into a closer union and form a real Federal State. The first was the pressure of growing nationalism in the neighboring countries. During the war of the Sonderbund, it became clear that unless some stronger bond was established the Confederation would fall apart and its fragments be absorbed by its neighbors. The second factor was an economic one. The industrial revolution, by altering the character of the Swiss economy, made some degree of centralization imperative. Yet the new order was accepted reluctantly, and the revised Constitution of 1874, which marked a further step in centralization, was carried only by 14½ Cantons as against 7½, and by 340,195 voices in favor over 198,013 voices against.

At first glance the Swiss Federal Constitution seems to be in many respects like that of the United States, on which it was consciously modeled. The Swiss Government, like the American, draws its authority from the cession made to it by the cantons of a part of their absolute sovereignty, and it is stipulated that it has no powers save those expressly named in the Constitution.

The Swiss legislature, the National Assembly, consists of two chambers. One, the Council of States, represents the cantons. It has forty-four members, two for each canton. The other, the National Council, represents the population. Every 22,000 Swiss citizens elect a representative to it. The executive power is vested in a body of seven men, the Federal Council.

These Councilors are elected by the National Assembly for a period of four years. Each of them holds an administrative portfolio, such as that of Foreign Affairs, or the Interior. They are paid by the Federal State a salary of 35,000 Swiss francs a year (about $7,000). Twice a year the National Assembly elects one of them as Chairman and another as Vice-Chairman. During his term of office this Chairman is called President of the Swiss Confederation. He has no particular privileges save that of presiding at the meetings of the Council and of representing the Confederation on public occasions. In practice this chairmanship, or Presidency, is given to each of the members of the Federal Council in turn. For this reason the average Swiss, although he may know who the members of the Council are, very often has no idea who happens to be President of the Confederation at any given moment.

There is a Federal Tribunal, whose twenty-four members are elected for a term of six years by the National Assembly. In practice they, too, are re-elected for as long as they wish to hold office.

Obviously the Swiss Government differs both from that of the United States and from those of other democracies such as France and England. Like the American Government it is non-parliamentarian, that is to say, the Executive power does not depend on, nor is it responsible to, the majority in the Legislature. If the policies sponsored by the Swiss Federal

Council are rejected by the National Assembly the Council does not retire, as does the Cabinet in France or in England. It goes calmly on, revising the measures it proposes according to the will of the National Assembly. In this respect it is like the Government of the United States. But the Swiss Executive, unlike that in the United States, is a council, of which no one member has more authority than the others. It is, moreover, chosen not by the people, but by the Legislature.

In comparing the Constitutions of these two countries a curious anomaly is evident. The Government of Switzerland is not nearly as liberal as that of the United States, but it is far more democratic. Political liberalism in the correct sense of the word means the protection of the rights of the individual by a limitation of the power of the State. The American Constitution-makers, acting on the theories of Montesquieu and other eighteenth-century philosophers, carefully separated the three functions of sovereignty, the legislative, the executive and the judicial, and created a system of checks and balances. The American Constitution contains, moreover, a declaration of rights.

The Swiss constitution-makers were less liberal. They created a powerful Legislature, which elects the executive officers (who have, therefore, none of the authority that comes from a popular election), and also the judges of the Federal Tribunal. These judges are chosen for a period of years, not for life, as are the members of the Supreme Court of the United States, and the Tribunal itself has no power to declare unconstitutional the laws passed by the National Assembly. That power the Assembly shares only with the people. There is no declaration of rights in the Swiss Constitution, although the right to freedom of conscience is specifically mentioned. So, too, are the rights to freedom of the press, of petition, of association and of protection against judicial abuses. Yet the Constitution itself forbids the creation of bishoprics on Swiss territory without the consent of the State and entirely prohibits the Society of the Jesuits from settling there. These provisions are not liberal.

Thus, constitutionally, the Swiss National Assembly has much more power than the American Congress. But political institutions do not always function as their makers intend. Strong in theory, the National Assembly has been in practice less important than the Federal Council. This executive body, which occupies the place of the President or Prime Minister in other democracies, actually possesses a large measure of stability and power. Bryce says of it: "Legally the servant of the legislature, it exerts in practice almost as much authority as do English, and more than do some French Cabinets. It is a guide as well as an instrument and often suggests as well as drafts measures." Its members are usually re-elected for long periods. From 1848 to 1936 there have been only fifty-six Federal Councilors. These men therefore acquire much experience and technique. They not only draft the laws but defend them both in the two legislative chambers and in committee. In addition, they administer the various departments of the Government.

Federalism is represented in the structure of this body. According to an unwritten law three of the Councilors always come respectively from Berne, Zurich, and Vaud. There is also as a rule one from Argovia. Another unwritten law provides that no more than five out of the seven Councilors shall be chosen from the German-speaking cantons.

Strong as the National Assembly and the Federal Council are, the Swiss Parliament does not possess a sovereignty as absolute as that of the French Chamber of Deputies under the Third Republic. Its power is limited in two ways: first, by the initiative and referendum; second, by the power which the cantons still hold.

William Rappard in his recent work on the Government of Switzerland defines the initiative as: "The right of a given fraction of the electorate to propose an amendment to the fundamental law." [1] This power may be used directly or indirectly. It is a right that most of the cantons, as well as the Federal State, have written into their Constitutions.

[1] Rappard, W.: *The Government of Switzerland.*

The referendum is of two kinds: optional and obligatory. The provisions of the Constitution of 1874 which are relevant to the optional referendum read: "The Federal Laws are submitted for the approval or rejection of the people, if thirty thousand qualified voters or eight cantons demand that they should be. The same rule applies to Federal ordinances when they are of general importance and not of an urgent character." In 1921 these provisions were extended to "International treaties concluded for an indefinite period or for more than fifteen years." Here, too, cantonal rights are safeguarded, for the Constitution can be amended only by the double majority of the electorate and the cantons. The legislative referendum, however, requires only the vote of the people.

Both the initiative and the referendum have been used very frequently in Switzerland since 1848, and particularly since 1900. There have been fifty constitutional referenda proposed, of which thirty-three were accepted; twenty-five constitutional initiatives, of which six were accepted; four parliamentary counter-proposals, of which three were accepted, and forty-four legislative referenda, of which fifteen were accepted. In all, 123 referenda and initiatives have been proposed, and fifty-seven accepted since 1848.

These forms of direct democracy have a double use. In the first place they are a powerful check on the legislative bodies. Any law passed by Parliament can be called in question and revoked by the people. The knowledge that the laws may have to run the gauntlet of public opinion makes the legislators cautious. On this subject Rappard says: "It is a well-known fact in Switzerland that the fear of popular repudiation is often a more potent factor in preventing the adoption by Parliament of certain legislative measures than the actual repudiation itself." [2]

In the second place the use of the initiative and referendum is highly educative. Far more than a vote cast once a year for an unknown candidate, it gives the elector a sense of personal responsibility. It obliges him to consider many problems for himself instead of leaving them to his representatives. There has been a tendency of late years in the United States to turn the representative system of government into one of mandates. The sending of telegrams and letters to senators and representatives, the efforts made to determine public opinion by the use of polls and straw votes, and the campaigns undertaken to bring the weight of this opinion to bear upon the legislators are moves in this direction. If government in the future is to be by absolute democracy instead of through representative institutions, if public opinion is to rule directly, the initiative and referendum furnish a method of determining that opinion which is both more accurate and more just than the hit-or-miss methods now employed.

[2] Rappard, W., *opus cit.*

There are, no doubt, dangers in the initiative and referendum, as there are in plebiscites. In the hands of demagogues acting upon a hot-headed and excitable people they might lead to revolution, or to extremist measures of all kinds. But the Swiss have shown themselves to be highly reasonable in the use of direct democracy, of which they have had a long experience. Frequently several attempts have been required to induce them to accept laws which they have at last adopted with satisfaction and profit. They have always rejected demagogic measures such as the socialistic "right to work" proposed in 1896, and the confiscatory capital levy proposed in 1922. They have also rejected most police measures which tended to limit the freedom of the individual, yet they have shown themselves at the polls to be willing to make great sacrifices for the public good. They have consented to extra taxation and to prolonged military service when these were needed. Under these circumstances, with a population so reasonable and so mature, the use of direct democracy is a valuable check upon the extremists and a barrier against dictatorship. Had a referendum been necessary to alter the Constitution, it is possible that neither Hitler nor Mussolini would have reached power legally, as they did.

The other check on the power of the Federal State is the continued vitality and influence of the cantons and of the communes. The 22 cantons, which are called "Sovereign" in the Constitution, have each a constitution of their own. These constitutions must be approved by the Federal Authority, which guarantees them. Three conditions are required for their acceptance. They must: (1) contain no provision contrary to those of the Federal Constitution; (2) assure the exercise of political rights according to republican —representative or democratic—forms of government; (3) have been accepted by, and be susceptible to, amendment at the demand of the absolute majority of the people. It is interesting to note that the wording of the Swiss Constitution implies a difference between representative and democratic governments.

The cantonal governments are at present of two types: the old Landesgemeinde and the representative forms. In the former the body of the voters, that is to say the whole male population over 21 years of age, assembles once a year in the public square to vote in person upon the laws and choose the administrators. They are the only existing instances of J. J. Rousseau's "Sovereign People." Only five of these Landesgemeinde still survive, and they are used by less than four per cent of the population. Moreover they are not today the practical governing bodies. The daily business of the State is carried on in these cantons by an elected council and by executive committees. Yet these Landesgemeinde are important as symbols of the age-old Swiss institutions, and they have considerable educational value. Rappard says of them: "From all over Switzerland fathers bring their children to witness the sight, unique in the annals of modern democracy and unequaled as an inspiring lesson of civic freedom and of devotion to the common country." [3] Jacob Dubs wrote on the same subject: "Here the unity of the country is physically represented,–administration, council, and people, spanned about by a single circle and upborne by a single thought. In this unity all political and social antagonisms are dissolved. . . . The thought of community, of the solidarity of all the interests of the people, of brotherhood under the same fatherland, wins power over the assembled multitude. . . . Orator and hearer lift each other to higher planes. There are moments when a silent awe takes possession of the crowd and the feeling wakes in them that they stand upon holy ground; that God is near them."

In the other cantons the government is vested in a Grand Council. These are in many ways the most important bodies in Switzerland, for in them much of the vitality of Swiss political life is to be found. Their members are numerous, no less so in the small cantons than in the large ones. These representatives draw no salary, merely a small compensation for attendance, but such posts are stepping-stones to political life. The executive power is vested in a Council of State, the members of which are elected by the people and administer the affairs of the canton.

[3] Rappard, W., *opus cit.*

The canton has retained certain rights which keep it in close contact with the people. It levies most of the direct taxes, it maintains law and order within its own borders, it builds and manages schools and universities. Only the Polytechnicum at Zurich is Federal. The canton determines the religious arrangements within its borders. The administration of justice is in its hands, for there is but one federal court, the Federal Tribunal, which has its seat in Lausanne, and its jurisdiction extends only to matters where the Federal law is concerned, to disputes between an individual and a canton, between cantons, or between one or more cantons and the central Government.

According to the Constitution the Federal Government derives its income solely from the following sources:

(a) The income from federal property.
(b) The proceeds of the federal customs levied at the Swiss frontier.
(c) The proceeds of the posts and telegraphs.
(d) The proceeds of the powder monopoly.
(e) Half of the gross receipts from the tax on military exemptions levied by the canton.
(f) The contributions of the cantons, which shall be determined by federal legislation with special reference to their wealth and taxable resources.

It was supposed in 1848 and 1874 that the Federal Government would be much poorer than the cantons since these were to levy both the direct taxes and those on alcohol. The contrary has been the case. With the development of Swiss industry and export trade the Federal Government has come to be much richer than the cantons, whose sources of revenue have tended to diminish. It is the Federal Government which now gives subsidies to the cantons in times of economic stress, to be used for relief. It might be supposed that this would tend to weaken the cantons but on the contrary it is generally agreed that the subsidies given by the Central State have had the contrary effect. This is because the cantons have kept the administration of this relief in their own hands.

The cantons retain the net profit of the Federal alcohol monopoly, although they allow it to be administered by the central Government. The Constitution obliges them to spend one-tenth of this amount in combatting alcoholism, and the cantonal governments have developed much imagination in circumventing this provision. Certain local administrators hit upon a particularly happy solution a few years ago; they spent the sum collected in spraying the vineyards of the district! The consumption of light wine, they declared, was the best way of preventing the consumption of brandies and whiskey.

To the average Swiss the "State" is not the Federal Government, but the government of the canton. He feels himself to be Vaudois, Genevese, Argovian, Valaisan before he feels himself to be Swiss, and it is to the nearby and familiar administration of his own canton that he turns for most things.

Loyalty to the cantons is an active feeling. Some years ago a Swiss millionaire left his native canton and moved to another, where the income tax was lower. He was frowned upon as unpatriotic quite as Americans would frown upon someone who went to live in Mexico for the same reason. The political parties themselves are to a large extent of cantonal origin and they are organized within the canton. Political issues are often purely local affairs and no nationwide elections such as the Presidential ones in the United States exist. The parties in the Federal Legislature are often more like alliances of cantonal groups than like true national parties. Candidates make use of the program of these national parties, but they do not as a rule depend upon them for support, but rather on their personal record and their cantonal popularity. This is an important fact in political life. The spoils system scarcely exists in Switzerland and the influence of the canton makes individual ability and integrity more important than services to the party. Cantonal politics diminish the anonymity of the single representative, lost in a huge political party, and lessen also the influence of party leaders.

Below the canton is the commune. Of these there are more than 3,000 in Switzerland, and some of them are very small, containing perhaps only some fifty souls. There are only four cities which have more than 100,000 inhabitants and but thirty-one in all have more than 10,000. The commune is the citizen's closest loyalty. It is, in fact, as a member of a commune that he is a citizen. In order to obtain Swiss nationality a foreigner must be accepted into one of these groups. The commune in which a Swiss citizen is born is permanently responsible for him. Even if he lives away from it for forty years, he may still return to it and demand support in sickness or in old age. There are several types of communes, just as there are of cantons. Some of the older ones possess corporate estates; pastures, woods or buildings. The income from these they use for the benefit of members of the community. In certain towns this corporate estate still gives all the burghers of the commune, that is to say its native-born members, not its *residents,* their firewood for the winter. Certain of the ancient burgher communes are held together largely by this common property in forests, meadows, or tillable land. Cases, however, are said to occur in which paupers, as to whose birthplace there is some doubt, are pushed to and fro from commune to commune and from canton to canton.

The organization of these communes is not unlike that of certain municipal governments in America. In many small places a town meeting is the principal organ of government, just as were the town meetings in the New England communities. In larger places the chief administrative authority is a communal council which is chosen either by the town meeting or by election.

There is great vitality in the Swiss communes. Some of them are in a measure spontaneous groups, for a commune may divide for some given purpose such as the founding of a new school, or the creating of a new water supply. Sometimes, too, several communes will unite for the sake of acquiring some advantages. In all such cases the communes tax themselves to pay for the expenses incurred. Some towns maintain hospitals and asylums, municipal playgrounds and baths, and the museums in which the Swiss delight to amass fragments of the beloved past and theaters are supported locally. A measure of state socialism exists in the cities in the form of municipal ownership and operation of water-works, street-car lines, gas and electric plants. These are usually very well run and therefore the policy of city or communal ownership is, on the whole, popular. The Swiss communes are among the best governed municipalities in the world.

Two facts are striking in Swiss political life. The first is the before-mentioned absence of outstanding individuals. It is not accidental that no great statesman, like Venizelos, Premier of a country even smaller than Switzerland, or Benes, leader of one scarcely larger, should be associated with the Confederation. In that country where the individual has so large a portion of freedom, he holds power only on the strict condition of sharing it. Neither the President of the Confederation nor the Mayor of a city enjoy an independent position.

Second, the State is ever the servant of the citizen, never his master. From the modest employee of the post office, who is always courteous and ready to serve and inform, to the President of the Confederation, who is usually a simple and unassuming person, far easier to meet and talk to than the smallest bureaucrat in an American business, the Swiss in public office is the public's servant. This is one reason why the State, like the Army, seems to the Swiss citizen to be really his own, to be his creation and his friend. In France the attitude of the average man towards anyone connected with the State is despairing. He knows that to these bureaucrats he is a mere worm, and that his chances of remedying any abuse are nil. The Swiss, on the contrary, feels that he can put things right. The officials are near. They are members, very often, of the same village or town. In any case they are not remote nor inaccessible. He probably knows his representative on the Grand Council. All this makes both government and democracy something very real to him. This is a great advantage, and it is due in part to the physical fact that the communities are small. Life in Switzerland, even in cities like Basel or Geneva, is intimate as compared with that of Paris, New York or London. Public opinion as regards individuals has more force, for the citizens know each other better. Moreover, most of the officials are appointed by the local authorities. In this respect it is interesting to compare Switzerland with France. In the cities of that highly centralized country, the prefect or sub-prefect is a mighty personage. He has a great deal of power, and plays a part in every activity, charitable, social or political. But he is the emissary of the Government in Paris, on which he and the whole hierarchy under him depend. The inhabitants of the community are well aware that he draws his authority from that remote power, which may protect him against them. In Switzerland, on the contrary, the prefect, representative of the Federal State, is a minor character, chiefly occupied with the customs.

In a recent study of Swiss bureaucracy two authors, one German and one American,[4] examine the reasons for the success of that hierarchy. They reject both the character of the people and the size of the nation as determining factors, and attribute success solely to organization. This would seem to be an exaggerated attitude, the more so since on an earlier page they admit that "the effectiveness of public opinion in regard to technical matters is limited to small communities." Both factors—the character of

[4] Friedrich, C. and Cole, T.: *Responsible Bureaucracy in Switzerland.*

the people and the size of the group—would seem to those who know Switzerland in its concrete reality to be important elements in the good government and administration of the country. The effect of institutions and of character are surely interdependent. It is a question of action and reaction.

There has been a very decided growth of centralization in Switzerland during the last fifty years, just as there has been in America. Apart from the influence of example, particularly that of Imperial Germany after 1870, two principal causes have been at work. The first is economic advantage. Here the story of the Swiss railroads is the most striking illustration. Before the creation of the Federal State, the problem of building a system of railways with no strong central authority to harmonize the wishes and needs of the cantons, or to coerce the recalcitrant, was very difficult. At the time of the first construction in 1852, the Federal Government took no responsibility, financial or administrative, for the railroads, although a strong minority favored at least a supervision by the central power. But when the tunnel of the Gothard was pierced, Germany and Italy, whose financial contribution was necessary, made assumption of responsibility by the Federal Government a condition of their aid. By 1898 opinion had already changed so much that the nationalization of the main lines of the Swiss railways was readily voted.

Industrial patents, the national resources in waterpower, internal navigation, and traffic itself, have all passed under Federal control, though not Federal ownership. The banking system was centralized in 1907. Of these facts Rappard says: "Technical progress engendered changed economic conditions, which in turn called for state intervention. As state intervention almost necessarily meant Federal intervention, the final result was centralization."

European wars have also caused Switzerland to increase its unity for the sake of national defense. Though much of the power conferred on the Federal government as a result of the first world war was withdrawn after 1919, some part of it was retained.

In the same way the needs of a modern military machine have tended to centralize the administration of the Army. Here, too, centralization has been relative, and it was resisted, but there has been an undoubted increase in Federal control since 1848.

More serious than these economic or technical factors in the growth of the central power is the increasing demand for State intervention in the social field. The evils of the industrial revolution, insecurity, bad conditions of work, poor housing, and so on, have tended to make the poorer classes feel that State intervention is necessary.

Switzerland has been progressive in its labor and social legislation. This has, of course, resulted in a certain amount of paternalism, and in the tendency to look on the State as a plum pudding, or a permanent Santa Claus. Such legislation has, therefore, increased the scope of federal power. But the cantons have retained much of the administration of these laws in their own hands, and so have limited the centralizing trend of social measures.

There are to some extent two Switzerlands, as the Swiss writer, Seippel, has declared that there are two Frances, divided more or less on confessional lines. The Catholic cantons after the failure of their effort at secession have continued to struggle to preserve as far as possible local autonomy, and to resist the encroachments of the Federal State. Their position may be compared with that of the southern states in America after the Civil War. But in Switzerland the federal idea and attachment to local independence was universal. Therefore the Catholic cantons found support in the "federal," that is to say, decentralizing policies of the conservative elements in the Protestant cantons.

The Constitution of 1848 and its revised edition of 1874 were the work of the more "radical" elements. These included primarily ultra-democratically minded and anti-clerical groups whose ideal was a state modeled on the Third French Republic. Such a state would, they felt, reflect more directly the will of the people and do more to help the poorer portions of the population. Some industrial interests, also, wanted a unified state because they believed that it would be more efficient in promoting the economic interests of the country at home and in the international field.

The struggle of the cantons against centralization is evident in certain provisions of the Constitution itself. Thus, Article 43 carefully stipulates the right of the Swiss citizen to settle in a canton not his own by origin, and Article 44 protects him against the arbitrary action of his own canton. Article 48 gives the Federal government authority to provide for the burial of persons from one canton who have died in another, and Article 53 gives the Federal Government the right to determine places of burial, so that every deceased person may be decently interred. Obviously these and other minor questions were subjects of dispute between the cantons and the Federal State. A series of provisions in Article 64 empowers the Confederation to make laws on various matters connected with commerce, copyright, collection of debts and bankruptcy.

The creation of a Federal State undoubtedly favored the growth of industry. With that growth an urban proletariat, divorced from the soil, developed in the larger cities, and in it socialism acquired considerable strength. Thus Geneva and Lausanne have had at one period a socialistic mayor. But socialism itself in Switzerland has been a foreign importation, and its force has been modified by local influences.

The Swiss political parties reflect these trends. For

many years the two principal ones were the Liberals, who were in fact conservatives, and the Radicals. These two parties came gradually to act more or less together and to dominate the political scene. It is interesting to note, however, that in the twentieth century not only the Socialists but the Catholic Conservatives have taken on increased importance. In 1935 these four parties together represented seventy-five per cent of the electorate.

Originally very individualistic, the Radical Party has made many concessions to the social-mindedness of the country and to the growth of socialism. It is still mildly anti-clerical and wholly democratic, but it favors a certain amount of state intervention to modify conditions of labor and improve the state of the country. The Socialist Party, while theoretically Marxian, has put much water in its wine. It is not revolutionary but evolutionary and democratic, therefore it caters to the peasant and the petty bourgeois. It is anti-Fascist, anti-capitalist, but not anti-militaristic.

The Catholic Party is anti-capitalist and also anti-socialist. It has been called theocratic. It advocates Christian co-operation and even a degree of corporatism. Its doctrines and program recall the encyclical *Rerum Novarum* of Leo XIII (1891).

All Swiss political parties are to a large extent social minded. None of them are actively revolutionary, with the exception of very small minorities on the left and on the right. The Swiss people are undoubtedly satisfied on the whole with their government and their State. The dangers from the outside to which they are exposed and the example of their neighbors have only increased their conviction that their own institutions are better than any others.

An obvious question arises in considering Switzerland. Why has the canton remained relatively vigorous in that country while in the United States of America the corresponding unit, the state, has lost so much vitality?

Federalism in the sense in which we have used it in this book, that is to say, the survival of local independence within an effective union, has obviously not resulted from the political institutions. The same Constitution, the same political forms in the hands of an undisciplined people might have given quite different results. They might easily have opened the doors to demagogical state control. On the whole the institutions of direct democracy, the initiative and referendum, tend rather to unify the population than to preserve cantonal authority and spirit.

The federal structure of the Swiss State, however, does correspond to the Swiss combination of conservatism and a progressive spirit. It has preserved local customs: language, religion, economic structure and so on, yet it has allowed progressive social and economic policies to develop. The Swiss have understood that mutual tolerance was mutually beneficial, that diversity is the secret of growth.

Konrad Falke, addressing the students of the University of Geneva in 1918, said: "The centralizing tendency has reached such a degree that now it seems to many that *in making freedom secure, freedom itself has been lost* . . . the centralizing idea is an idea eminently un-Swiss because it is un-free; it is the father of imperialism, and the most terrible thing about it is that today the whole world has fallen under its sway." It is probable, as an authority on Switzerland has pointed out, that if they were alone in the world the Swiss would still be satisfied with a loose league, leaving almost complete sovereignty in the hands of the cantons. The one justification for centralization is that it makes possible the greatest amount of decentralization within the country.

So long as the Federal Government confines its activities to economic measures and to problems involving international action, and leaves political, social and administrative matters in local hands, the principle of Federal liberty is safe-guarded. For instance, the nationalization of the railroads was normal and harmless; the unification of the penal code was much more debatable.

Democracy is an instrument, a method of securing the freedom and welfare of the people. As such it has great advantages. In the first place it is flexible. Persons and programs can be changed legally, without resorting to violence. In a successful democracy, the government will be in close contact with the people, who take part in its origin and renewal. Diversity and varied types of life must be tolerated in a democratic State, for the existence of an opposition is essential to it. A testimony to this truth came from the mouth of the German Chancellor, Brüning, at the time when the Nazi Party withdrew in a body from the Reichstag. Someone congratulated him on being rid of so troublesome a faction. "No," he said, "I prefer to have them in the Chamber. A vigorous opposition is necessary for democratic government."

Democracies, however, are not always liberal. Majorities may oppress minorities. Vast impersonal governments, remote from the electors whom they supposedly represent, may be the result of the "one man, one vote" system. A socialistic bureaucracy may even be the end-process of democracy in the modern mechanized and materialistic world. That is one reason why the makers of the American Constitution were so careful to safeguard the rights of the individual and to limit the power of the representative bodies themselves.

In Switzerland it is the local groups, the cantons and communes, which safeguard the rights and liberties of the citizens, which secure for them the variety and diversity that give life concrete value. In this way monotony and standardization, which are the curse of our modern monster States, are avoided.

Federalism no doubt implies equilibrium and struggle, but that is the characteristic of a wholesome political life. There are no minorities in the totalitarian States; they are like immense frozen political deserts.

Danger to the liberty of the individual comes today in large part from the very size of the modern State; in it the central government is so remote that the individual can not make himself felt. In addition, an enormous and anonymous bureaucracy tends to be irresponsible, and the separation of powers does nothing to correct this. The three powers may check each other, but they do not bring the State nearer to the average man, as does federalism. In the cantons and communes the individual does count. He knows and can control in a measure the local government which he has created. Centralized democracy tends to concentrate power and diffuse responsibility, passing the buck becomes a technique. Federalism divides and dilutes power, but it fixes personal responsibility.

The Swiss State has given proof that variety and decentralization do not necessarily imply weakness. Out of a common will to remain together, out of a common ideal of life, a national spirit quite as strong as that to be found in forceably unified States has grown. The will to preserve their diversity has enabled the Swiss to act together in all the major crises of history. Today in an hour of trial greater than any it has had to meet since the days of its birth the political structure of Switzerland appears to be adequate to bear the burden that is laid upon it. Federalism is proving itself not a liability but an asset.

V. THE PEOPLE; ONE YET MANY

A LEGEND of the Rhône Valley says that while God was making the world, Saint Peter was very troublesome. He followed his Master about criticizing all that He did. Nothing pleased him. One country was too large, one too small, one was too hilly, another too flat. At last the Lord said to him: "Since you don't like what I have created, take this piece of earth and make a land that is to your taste."

Eagerly Saint Peter went to work, resolved to make the finest country in the world. He piled up mountains that touched the sky, and dug valleys so deep that they seemed bottomless. In them he put swift torrents whose voices could be heard even on the peaks. Everything was superlative. Proudly he showed this beautiful land to the Lord.

"Humph," said the Deity, "very nice. But what about man? How can he grow his crops on those steep rocks, or float his boats down those rushing rivers?"

Saint Peter was abashed, but he thought awhile.

"I will put soil on the rocks and pin it down with pine trees," he said.

But the rain fell and the winds blew upon the steep slopes and washed away both soil and pines, leaving only the naked rock. Saint Peter looked ruefully at his handiwork.

"Never mind," said God. "You have made the land but I myself will make the men to live in it and all will be well."

So He made a man sturdy and long of breath who could climb the mountains without fatigue, a man with a keen eye and a sure foot who would not fall into the precipices, a lean man, able to thrive and be contented with little. To him He gave a faithful heart, so that he would never be happy away from his mountains. He was the Swiss mountaineer.

For most Americans this mountaineer is the typical Swiss, and so, indeed, in some respects he is. Yet other types exist, for there is as much variety among the people of Switzerland as there is in their scenery.

Racially, like all modern Europeans, they are a complex mixture, for the country has been a land of passage and a very ancient site of civilization. From the dawn of pre-history men have inhabited its valleys. Before the bronze age a mysterious race of lake dwellers built their water-kept homes on the shores of the Swiss lakes. Remains of the piles which ten thousand years ago supported these miniature Venices may still be glimpsed sometimes through the still waters of the Leman when the lake is low.

Caesar found a Celtic people, the Helvetians, settled in the land. Traces of their language are left in place-names ending in a silent "z" or "x," like Tolochenaz, or Chamonix. Rome conquered and civilized Switzerland, and it became for her a corridor leading to Gaul and to the German frontier. The original Roman milestones still stand in some places beside the modern highway. Along the roads where marched the legions sprang up such cities as Aventicum, whose wide ruins surround the little town of Avenches.

In the period of the barbarian invasions a series of Teutonic tribes, Franks, Burgundians, Alemanni, poured over the land, mingling with the Gallo-Roman population. At a later day the Saracens came up through the valleys. Ruins of the towers built against them exist on Lake Geneva and along the Rhône, and they have left signs of their passage in place-names such as that of the Castle of La Sarraz.

Among the Swiss of today some pure Celtic and some definitely Moorish types can be found, but the dominant physical strain, even in French Switzerland, is Germanic. The people resulting from this mixture are not beautiful. They lack the soft-eyed grace of the Italians, the fineness of feature of the French, but they are wholesome. Even in the cities they have kept the aspect of country folk, the women rosy-cheeked and broad-hipped, the men rough-hewn and strong.

The painter Hodler in his tremendous picture of the Battle of Marignano has shown the typical Swiss pikeman: heavy, bull-necked and thick featured, grim and dogged even in defeat. Something of this power is still to be seen in the peasant of German Switzerland. He is essentially a fighter.

There are as many tongues among the Swiss as there are races. Seventy-one per cent of the population speak German, twenty per cent speak French, six per cent Italian, and one and one-tenth per cent Romanche. Each of the German-speaking cantons has its own dialect. These dialects are thicker and more guttural than the true German and some of them contain strange words interpolated from other languages. For instance, the Bernese word for a watch is "skeloretti" which comes from the French "quelle heure est-il." The Swiss, however, are very much attached to these dialects and they are used even in society in preference to the German which is taught in the schools. At a fashionable wedding in Basel the host was heard to say to some of his guests: "In my house we speak French or German Swiss—never German." In the Grisons another language of Latin origin, the Ladin, exists, and in the Valais there is a French dialect which is spoken by the peasants. Switzerland, in short, recalls the tower of Babel.

Two churches are supported by the State: the Roman Catholic and the Swiss National Church, which is Calvinist. Fifty-seven per cent of the population is Protestant and forty-one per cent Catholic. The religious and linguistic frontiers do not correspond, however. The French-speaking cantons are in majority Protestant, but a part of Fribourg, Valais and the Bernese Jura are Catholic, and so is the Ticino. Of the German cantons some belong to one and some to the other of the two religions.

The State supports the church to which the majority of the population in each canton belongs, but the minority faith has churches of its own which are tolerated and even encouraged. In some of the Protestant communities the inhabitants make great efforts to help the priests and the Catholic churches, in order that those who come from the neighboring cantons may find their own religion and their own customs. There are a great quantity of sects in Switzerland: Lutherans, Old Catholics, Darbysts, Mormons, and others. But the total number of their adherents is very small, and the population is almost entirely divided into the two major groups.

In addition to these various races, tongues and religions, wide differences of occupation in the several regions have increased the human variety. There is no standardization. What is remarkable is that proximity has not created likeness. On the contrary, the smaller the group the more it tends to affirm its own individual traits. The Swiss are proud of their differences and tell many stories at each other's expense. It is said that three men, one from Geneva, one from Berne and one from Lausanne, went out to gather snails. The shrewd and active Genevese brought back twenty, the man from Berne had only ten, but when the Vaudois came along, he had none. "What happened?" asked the others. "I did catch one," was the answer, "but he escaped me!"

These differences were once rivalries and hatreds. Genevans, Bernese, Zurichois, Balois, Valaisans, were not always allies. The Vaudois, who today celebrate the Swiss victory over Charles the Bold at Morat, forget that their ancestors fought under the banners of the proud Duke. Valaisans show you spots in the pass called the *Pas de L'Ours,* the Bear's Step, where their ancestors put sentinels to watch against the coming of the people of the Bear, and a meadow in the valley where the two races fought is still called the Bloody Pasture. Today racial hatreds are forgotten, but the differences remain.

Many mountain villages can be reached only on mule-back over narrow trails and lie at four or five hours' distance from the nearest center. Some, older than the cities in the valley, were built by men who took refuge on the heights from the persecutions of the decaying Roman Empire. Yet even in these regions there are few, if any, solitary habitations. The life of the Swiss peasant is, in fact, communal, and the loneliness of western farms in America scarcely exists. In such communities the ideas of liberty on the one hand and of neighborly co-operation on the other are ever present.

In certain parts of the Valais the local spirit is still so strong that people from other cantons are looked on with mistrust as strangers. This narrow provincialism leads to feuds and vendettas of the kind that are to be found in the Kentucky mountains, and the police are powerless to stop them. Not many years ago these feuds were fought out in blood. Even now there are occasional shootings, but as a rule quarrels are less violent. In a small village called Chermignon there are two "musics," or bands, which play at all the festivities of the neighboring regions. The rule is that each must play the same number of tunes, in order that there may be no jealousy. When a few years ago one band exceeded its quota a riot followed and the offending "music" ended by barricading itself in a house and defiantly playing all night.

Like most mountaineers, the men of these remote regions are superstitious. They live too close to nature, with its caprices and dangers, not to feel the mystery of life. The writer, C. F. Ramuz, whom we have already quoted, has painted in *La Grande Peur dans la Montagne* a remarkable picture of peasant life in the high mountains. A Greek sense of ineluctable destiny, of the strength of blind forces, finds expression in this work.

Very unlike the mountaineers are the dwellers in

the milder regions of lakes and plateaux. The Vaudois, for instance, is an easy-going fellow, fond of good living, and especially of the white wine which grows on the terraced slopes of his country. Cellar parties, in which wines of every year and vintage are tasted, are his favorite pastime. Though reputed slow and heavy, he has a wit which is half naïveté, half shrewdness. A Vaudois who visited the tomb of Napoleon and looked at the massive sarcophagus of black marble under which lie the Imperial ashes, remarked: "Poor Napoleon! He did so like to come and go!" A truly Swiss résumé of the Napoleonic epic. Upon this easy-going nature Calvinism was grafted, and the Vaudois is uneasily aware of the Divinity, who is a jealous God. A peasant from Lavaux, visiting his ruined vineyards after a hailstorm, shook his fist at the sky. "I won't name Anyone," he exclaimed angrily, "but this is disgusting!"

The German Swiss have a different type of humor. They love to play practical jokes and to abuse each other. The favorite accusation is theft—probably because the Swiss are extremely honest and there is very little thievery in the country. In passing from one canton to another, it is said, the locomotive engineer always looks back to make sure that no one has stolen the last coach of the train. This, they declare, is why there are so many hair-pin turns on the railways.

In spite of all these local differences and peculiarities, certain traits are characteristically Swiss. Simplicity of life and a jealous spirit of equality are among them. They are the old civic tradition of the cantons. The Swiss Government bestows no honors or decorations upon its citizens and does not allow those who serve it to accept them from other countries. Swiss families which have titles never use them when they are at home.

The contrast between rich and poor, the gulf between classes, is less evident in Switzerland than in other countries. It has been said that it is the worst place in the world in which to be rich and the best in which to be poor. This is partly because the social-minded communities do much for the needy and for the public at large, but also because wealth is widely distributed. There are relatively few large fortunes and also few desperately poor people in the country. Except in the larger cities the difference in the way of life between the middle and the lower classes is not marked. Many professional people, many good old families live more frugally than the rich peasants of Vaud or Berne. For instance, a lady who is half-owner of one of the finest feudal castles in Switzerland, one which has belonged to her family for two hundred and fifty years, not only manages the farm and vineyards herself but has been known to sit in the market place and sell her vegetables side by side with the country women of the neighborhood.

In some mountain regions possessions are few—

they may not even include pewter or earthenware dishes, yet the people have something of their own: a chalet, a bit of pastureland, a few cows. They own property, be it ever so little, and they do not feel "poor," for they have security and an established place in the community.

There is a deliberate effort on the part of the rich and powerful not to be different from others. Not only does everybody travel third class in the trains, but the modest bicycle is very popular. There is one for every fifth inhabitant in Geneva. It is not considered good taste to make a show of luxury, and women of the best society dress so simply that they look like superior governesses. Strangers are often amazed to find that the shabby man whom they met in a railway carriage or saw plodding along a country road is a rich banker or landowner.

The Swiss mistrust too great courtesy and charm of manner. What the French call "la bonne grace"—graciousness—seems to them insincere. They greatly value frankness—which often means an inclination to tell unpleasant truths bluntly. The highest praise that they can bestow is to say of someone that he or she is "so simple."

The treasures of delicate porcelain and heavy old silver which many Swiss homes contain are never displayed; they are tucked away in a top cupboard or kept locked in chests, to be taken out only on the occasion of family celebrations. In a modest house near Lake Leman there was a remarkable collection of Persian miniatures, brought back from abroad by an ancestor who served the British East India Company. The family was well aware of their value and interest, yet they were not kept in the parlor, but hung on the walls of the upstairs bedrooms. To have exhibited them would have been considered pretentious—a heinous offense in Swiss eyes.

There is more parade of luxury in semi-international cities like Geneva, Zurich or Basel, yet even there wealth has a certain secrecy. For example, the houses of the old Geneva aristocracy, on the steep and narrow Rue des Granges, have starkly plain façades that give no hint of the sumptuous abodes within.

These austere façades, hiding a richness and variety of life rigorously kept for an inner circle of friends and relatives, are symbolic of Swiss character, of its self-sufficiency, its mistrust of pretentious semblance, its dignity—and also its narrowness. They explain why Americans know so little of the real Switzerland, why tourists as a rule see only Alps and hotels and often fail to discover that the Swiss are anything more than guides and hotel-keepers.

Another Swiss trait is the remarkable mixture of a progressive spirit with prudent conservatism and a deep respect for tradition. The Swiss citizen is a man of good sense, he is highly practical, and is eager to profit by all new things which are useful. He is, therefore, adaptable and can change with the times. He has in many respects adjusted himself much better to modern conditions than his quicker-witted Latin neighbors. Like the American, he has a great interest in science, particularly in its practical results. The Swiss are excellent engineers—they built spiral tunnels long before these were known in America; they are fond of machinery and excel at making it. They have studied the scientific aspects of their country, its geógraphy, geology, and fauna with keen interest and have a great faculty of observation. They are always ready to try new inventions, new methods.

Many practical and scientific tendencies are evident in Swiss daily life. Modern methods of hygiene were in use in Switzerland before they became popular elsewhere. Sun-bathing is widely practiced and a characteristic sight is that of day laborers in summer stripped to the waist, their torsos as brown as chocolate.

Swiss clinics and sanitoria are renowned for the excellent care given in them, and people come from all parts of the world to consult certain famous Swiss doctors. Such were the psychiatrist, Jung, the gynecologist, Muret, and many others, including that great surgeon, the late César Roux. The latter was what is called a "character," and a very Swiss one. He was of peasant origin and his students still speak with admiration of his flow of similies and illustrations drawn directly from nature. He was almost as well known for his willful simplicity and his fierce disinterestedness as for his astonishing skill. He disapproved of fee-splitting and he had his own method of dealing with it. When foreign doctors would call him in to a consultation in Paris, Berlin or Rome, expecting to share a large honorarium, he would calmly charge the patient five francs and a third-class return trip ticket to Lausanne. It is told of him that a Duchess came to consult him and was bidden to take a chair and wait with the other patients. When she tried to make Doctor Roux understand that she was, after all, the Duchess of Blank he coolly rejoined, "Very well, Madame. In that case, take two chairs." Whether the story is true or not, its democratic bluntness delights the Swiss.

Switzerland is the country of out-of-doors and of health, *par excellence*. Its cities are small enough to make the country, the lakes and mountains, always accessible. The Swiss use their land to the utmost for pleasure as well as for profit. They have made it a playground not only for Europe but for themselves. That is one of their permanent sources of contentment. There is no village, however tiny, on any Swiss lake which has not its beach, and cities such as Lausanne, Geneva and Zurich have several elaborate bathing establishments. In summer the lakes are dotted with sails, for nearly every inhabitant has a boat of sorts in which to idle and dream—or fish. Local regattas are great events in the holidays, and the Swiss were long the champions of the world in the sport of sailing a boat.

They are an active people who prefer to scramble over their country rather than to ride through it, and the seemingly wild and lonely mountain regions are full of alpinists in summer and skiers in winter. Summer chalets are tucked away at the foot of glaciers and peaks, for in spite of their love of economy most comfortably-off Swiss people prefer to spend their vacations in their own country rather than in nearby France or Italy, where life is two or three times cheaper.

Every Saturday and holiday, vast crowds of men and women, knapsack on back and alpenstock in hand, pile into the trains, intent on climbing. Children so young that they have to be helped and old people whom one would expect to find sitting by the fire go along. The sturdiness of Swiss legs and the length of Swiss breath are remarkable at every time of life.

Alpinism has become the profession of one group of people, the guides. These men exhibit some of the most characteristic Swiss traits. Thanks to their skill the mountains have become for them a means of livelihood. To exploit this resource, however, they need endurance, sobriety and judgment, as well as courage and integrity. Many are the true stories of guides who have died rather than leave their "monsieur."

The keen enjoyment of their own land and its pleasures which is so widespread in Switzerland is an important fact. It has helped to create the independence and contentment with little which are vital factors in Swiss economy.

Another progressive Swiss trait is cleanliness. It is amusing when one crosses the frontier from France to see how regularly on one side the beds will be good and the foods delicious but dirt will be accepted as an inevitable though regrettable fact, whereas in the first Swiss village across the line the beds will be hard and the food simple and monotonous, but every sanitary arrangement will be impeccable.

Love of order is innate in most Swiss people and it may be carried almost to the length of regimentation. In the great white boats, like huge swans, which ply about the lake of Geneva, *Entrance* and *Exit* are plainly marked in front of the ticket office, but when crowds of French people get on at Evian a certain number usually rush hopefully to the Exit, expecting to squeeze in and save half a minute. The big, good-natured Swiss guard always stops them firmly, and he has been heard to say in tones of mild remonstrance: "Go in by the Entrance. No disorder here. You're in Switzerland now."

Swiss homes are, as a rule, well heated and supplied with a certain amount of modern equipment. In prosperous districts the peasants would not buy a house without central heating and electric lights. Owing to the abundant supply of water power, electricity is cheap. Not only are ninety-nine per cent of Swiss houses equipped with it but even in the remoter and poorer districts it is often used for cooking.

We have noted how often old buildings are still in use. The castle becomes the Town Hall or the Arsenal, the old arcades shelter shops and homes. In Geneva the walls of Gondebaud, King of the first Burgundian dynasty, so whitewashed and scrubbed that they have lost all look of age, fit snugly into more recent constructions and serve to buttress a public square. Sometimes extreme cleanliness gives a slightly theatrical look to these relics of the past. Tourists who visit Morat, where all the ramparts with their towers and gates are intact, have been known to doubt whether these were real or only a stage setting, and Chillon and the dungeon of Bonnivar have become so spic and span that Americans sometimes declare that if only the cuisine had been adequate the prisoner would have had little cause for complaint.

These are visible forms of a progressive civilization, but others are equally important. Among them is education. Political federalism implies a large number of varied cultural centers, and democracy on a small scale, perhaps all democracy worthy of the name, implies a strong interest in education. The Swiss are called a nation of hotel-keepers, but their success in this profession, which after all employs only a limited number of people, scarcely justifies such a rash generalization. It would be more accurate to say that every Swiss citizen is something of a pedagogue. This does not refer only to the governesses, who, like hotel-keepers, are supposed to represent Switzerland abroad, nor does it mean the large number of teachers and schoolmasters in the various secondary institutions, commercial, technical, and agricultural, nor the university professors and heads of private institutions of learning that are to be found in Switzerland. There is more than that. *Every* Swiss is more or less a pedagogue because in so small a country, where men are so closely packed together, and where order depends entirely on the discipline of the citizens, everybody by sheer force of circumstances becomes at once the teacher and the pupil of his neighbor. The Swiss is a great giver of advice. He likes to explain the handling of an instrument, to tell you the names of the Alps that you see, the history of his canton, what he is doing and what you ought to do. He explains with a technical earnestness that is full of pith and with a moral earnestness that easily becomes pedantic and "preachy." Like the Germans, but with more humor, and above all without desire to impress or compel you, solely from curiosity as to facts and from human sympathy, the Swiss is didactic.

What are the results for Switzerland itself of this pedagogical tendency? A few facts will give an idea of them. The percentage of illiterates is the lowest in the world. Primary schooling, from six to thirteen years of age, as in the United States, is free and obligatory. The diploma which is given at the end of this schooling gives the right to secondary education, and the studies in the "gymnase" lead to the "Baccalaureat," which admits to the university and to the advanced technical schools.

Unlike the American system, however, Swiss education is not entirely democratic. The primary schools do not all prepare for the higher grades that lead to the university; if the student is to obtain his "Bachot" he must be placed early in a school where Latin and Greek are taught.

The primary school occupies the lives of children —that is to say keeps them seated and motionless—for five hours every day from 6-13 years old. It is one of the fundamental Swiss institutions of the nineteenth and twentieth centuries. There it is that young Switzerland learns to be disciplined, respectful of the average, mistrustful of all that is out of the normal, either high or low—learns in short, "equality." It must be admitted that if Switzerland is a land of liberty it is also a land of intolerance towards the best and the worst—the head and the tail of the class. Perhaps democratic liberty must be paid for at this price. The best, if they really have a vigorous nature, succeed in spite of everything, if not in their own country, at least by the roundabout way of going abroad. But the weakest have a sad lot; they lower the averages, and are looked down on.

Perhaps Switzerland owes its limited number of paupers to the fact that extreme poverty and illiteracy are simply not accepted or considered possible there. In other European countries poverty has a kind of almost mystical distinction. There is a quantity of romantic literature that deals with Italian beggars—but in Switzerland no one feels they have the right to fall too low. A kind of general conspiracy brings men back to the average, willy-nilly. Genius and wealth hide themselves, imbecility or poverty try to seem to be at the normal level, and everyone helps them to do so.

The Swiss teacher is a sort of regulator of democratic life. To say of anyone in Switzerland that he wants to distinguish himself is an insult. This fact is regrettable from the spiritual and intellectual point of view, but it is a guarantee against tyranny.

There are many private schools of various types in Switzerland, some dedicated to the most modern psychological investigations, and others confessional, but the students in these institutions are all obliged to pass the same final examinations as those required in the public schools.

Characteristically, Switzerland has seven universities for a country of less than four and a half million inhabitants. This would be far too many for the needs of Switzerland itself, but a quantity of students come to them from foreign countries. Each of the French Swiss cantons has its university. It is not physical needs which are responsible for this, since Fribourg, Lausanne, Neuchâtel, and Geneva are little more than an hour apart by train. Were these institutions to fuse, the resulting one would be more prosperous and powerful than any of them can now hope to be, but this would be quite contrary to Swiss tradition and spirit. Each university is a permanent cultural center, each has its own past, its own tradition and character. That of Fribourg is a center of Catholic and French civilization; that of Geneva is at once Calvinist and international; that of Neuchâtel specializes in the law; and that of Lausanne represents a sort of Vaudois "nationalism," which can perhaps be explained by the fact that Vaud is both the largest and most predominantly peasant—therefore the most conservative—of the French cantons. As to Germanic Switzerland, it has the Universities of Basel (the oldest one of all), of Zurich, of Berne. The Federal Polytechnical School at Zurich, the Engineering School at Lausanne and the School of Commercial Studies at St. Gall rank as universities.

Finally the most striking aspect of Swiss progressiveness is the sense of social responsibility. The conviction of a mutual duty between citizens manifests itself in a keen interest in charity and social welfare. This is the avocation of many men and women of standing. In fact, not to be active in "good works" would be socially damning in the best Swiss circles.

Countless committees, boards, clubs and societies exist in every small town, to organize and support hospitals, clinics, kindergartens, and many other institutions. For instance, in Morges, which has about 4,000 inhabitants and is only twelve miles from the city of Lausanne, there is an infirmary for the sick and aged poor, a preventorium [1] and a home for feeble-minded children. There are several clinics, a visiting nurse, a prohibition restaurant, and a society for giving coffee to the women who sell vegetables in the streets on market day. Each of the several churches has charities of its own. In fact in some of the more prosperous communities in happier times there scarcely seemed to be enough unfortunates to absorb the energy of the charitably minded.

In a country which is that of J. J. Rousseau and Pestalozzi it is not astonishing that child welfare—puericulture, as it is called—should be very popular. Clinics for pre-natal care as well as kindergartens and preventoria abound. In the study of feeble-mindedness and insanity, too, the Swiss have shown great interest. There are an astonishing number of hos-

[1] Preventoria are homes for pre-tubercular children.

pitals for the psychologically sick, for the Swiss give medical and institutional care to many persons who in other countries would be left at large in the community.

Side by side with this modern spirit there is much conservatism in Swiss character. In so small a country, where a part of the land is uninhabitable and the rest over-populated, where all men are neighbors, where the soil is often barren and raw materials almost non-existent, everything must be used to the utmost and all that the ancestors have built must be carefully preserved. The meticulous cleanliness of the houses and the streets, the taste for good workmanship and for durable and well-finished objects, the hedges and walls which separate each holding so strictly, even the civic discipline which is at once rigorous and spontaneous, can be explained by the physical needs which weigh on each citizen and oblige him both to live very close to others and not to allow any of the goods so hardly won to be lost. The universal fear of waste, the conservatism which, though sometimes narrow, adds to life the dimension of historical depth, is certainly what distinguishes most sharply a country like Switzerland from one like America, where everything has been so abundant, so easy, that economy and the preservation of old things could well seem to be mere avarice or useless luxury.

Miserliness is rather laughed at than despised in

Switzerland. It is said of the stingy, with a smile, that when they boil eggs they send the broth to the poor. Prudence also has come to be almost second nature. Two men from a lakeside village were out sailing when a tremendous gale came up and seemed about to capsize them. "Ought we not to say a little prayer?" one suggested, as the boat heaved far over in the wind, but the other replied cautiously: "Better not attract attention!"

In Swiss homes the same careful conservatism is evident. Kitchen and bathroom will be ultra-modern but the drawing room remains Louis XVI. This gives a comforting sense of continuity. The Revolution which in France dispersed and scattered goods and people, in Switzerland destroyed little—to the great benefit of beauty-lovers of today.

In the Château of Wufflens near Lausanne there is a set of Louis XIV furniture. It was re-covered with the finest petit-point tapestry at the time of Louis XVI, and a painting on the wall shows the Chatelaine of that period and her daughters embroidering the very chairs on which her descendants now sit and embroider others.

A typical house in Morges was built upon a vast two-story cellar. The family fortune came from vineyards and when a new home was needed it was simply erected on top of the deep vaults where the great stone wine-presses stood. This same house had the first bathroom in that region. It consisted of a corrugated zinc tub which was covered with a clean sheet for each bath and was filled with hot water brought from the kitchen stove in pails. When later a new bathroom was built it occurred to no one to do away with the old—it was kept for "second class" emergency baths. In that house, too, the spinning wheel at which members of the family remember seeing their grandmother work stands in one corner of the parlor, and some of the linen still actually in use was made of thread spun on it in the eighteenth century.

In the Valais where the foreign service was popular the old uniforms are religiously kept, and they are worn in the procession on the feast of Corpus Christi. Every uniform of eighteenth-century Europe, French, Spanish, Austrian, Prussian, Neapolitan, can be seen on that day.

Another aspect of Swiss conservatism is a tendency to follow the same trade or profession from generation to generation. Skilled artisans such as watchmakers are the product of a long tradition. There are peasant families where a knowledge of how to care for the vineyards and make the wine is handed on from father to son. Even in the professions men are apt to become clergymen or lawyers or doctors according to what their forefathers were.

The basis of Swiss conservatism is the strength of the family bond. That is true in every walk of life, from peasant to aristocrat. In the Catholic cantons the family is, of course, vigorously supported and encouraged by the Church. People take pride in having as many children as possible, and families of fifteen or even twenty are not unknown. But the influence of family is nearly as great in Protestant Switzerland. Many grown men still obey their fathers almost as though they were boys, and submit to a discipline which seems astonishing to Americans.

The Swiss family is a sort of close corporation for mutual aid, within which, whether there is affection or not, there is great solidarity. Enormous sacrifices are made for it. Women will sell their jewels, men will mortgage their homes to save a hated cousin from bankruptcy. There is prudence as well as duty in this, for in Switzerland, as in most old and highly organized societies, *who* as well as *what* a man is counts, and the good or ill repute of his family may be of vital help or hindrance to him.

This family comprises more than the mere relatives; it is a clan that includes uncles and aunts, cousins, second-cousins, and in-laws. At a Swiss wedding a hundred people will often call each other kin. Switzerland is the land of cousins, for there has necessarily been much intermarriage in these small communities. A few years ago a genealogist of Geneva amused himself by establishing the exact relationship between Jean Jacques Rousseau and a number of prominent Swiss people of the day. All of them, he found, had some degree of kinship with the philosopher, but many of them were far from pleased to know it!

The family is a restraint on individualism and it may be something of a tyranny. It involves many duties such as visits to a great collection of elders. In a family known to one of the authors there were seven ladies more than eighty years old who had to be visited on every occasion. They were not only the family censors but also the archivists, the keepers of family secrets, family genealogies, stories and traditions. There are interminable family dinners and solemn family councils of war. In some families there are even trust funds held in common for all the members and to which all the members contribute. Family opinion must always be reckoned with, and young people who are at odds with their parents or elders are seriously handicapped. They will be looked on askance by most people even if they have some justification, for the principle of revolt is considered dangerous. But, tyranny or not, the enduring power of the family is an essential part of the stability of Swiss civilization. It is a kind of social cement which holds the community together.

Partly because of the importance of the family, Swiss society, though it is simple in its habits, is not democratic in the American sense. There is probably no milieu in the world harder to penetrate than the patrician groups in small Swiss cities. Neither beauty, wit, wealth nor fame can procure an entry into these circles; but, on the other hand, those who "belong" are looked after and treated with consideration even if they are old, poor and stupid. This makes a society which is certainly not amusing—it would scorn to be so—but which is very solid. In it the idea of mutual responsibility has persisted, and from the point of view of the community this is not an evil. To be of good family and to maintain the reputation of one's ancestors is usually to be a good citizen.

In this society many descendants of the once powerful oligarchies still exist. Sturdy and prolific, these families, although they have no legal rights or privileges, are often highly respected and wield a considerable influence in their own communities.

That there should be a Swiss aristocracy astonishes Americans, yet it is one of the oldest in Europe. Both the Habsburgs and the House of Savoy originated in Switzerland. More than one modest-seeming Swiss family has had the right, won centuries before, to attend without invitation the jealously guarded Imperial court in Vienna. It is said that a simple-minded member of one of these families took advantage of his privilege to go to a court ball. He was presented to the Emperor Francis Joseph and reminded him that their families had come from the same part of the world, implying that his own had once been the richer and more powerful of the two. "No doubt," smiled the Emperor, "but you will admit that mine has done much better for itself!"

In France, the nobles whose function had been to carry arms and to defend the land, lost their social significance when the King created a professional army instead of the feudal levies. As centralization increased they were attracted to Versailles and became mere courtiers. This set them apart from the bourgeoisie and the people. Moreover, French law did not allow a noble to engage in any sort of trade or commerce, or to marry, except by special dispensation, the daughter of a "roturier." In Switzerland there was no King or court. Therefore the nobles remained on their land. They were in contact with the burghers and with the people, and often took part with them against the Emperor. For instance, a d'Erlach, member of a noble family of Berne, commanded the Swiss at the battle of Laupen. The Swiss nobles were prevented by no royally enforced law or custom from marrying into the rich and powerful burgher families of the towns.

In the growth and government of the cantons the nobility played a great part. The Diesbachs, the Wattevilles, the Bonstettins furnished Berne with many of its leaders and administrators in the days of its power. They and other leading families gave bailiffs to the subject provinces and were sent as representatives of the city abroad.

The Swiss nobility had many affiliations in foreign

lands and so kept up the Swiss tradition of internationalism. The de Salis, a powerful family of the Grisons, and the de Blonays have in the past intermarried with ruling families. Others took service with foreign sovereigns. An Abbé de Watteville was Grand d'Espagne, French Marquis and Pasha. Friederich de Salis was the almoner of Henry IV of France; Andreas de Salis, vicar of the Valteline, was a secret agent of Louis XIV. Instances might be multiplied. In Neuchâtel many aristocrats took service with the King of Prussia, who was the nominal sovereign of the principality. The de Pourtales are a notable instance of a family whose internationalism has lasted to our own day. One of them helped in the last century to found Colorado Springs, another was German ambassador to Petrograd, while many served with the French army.

With the growth of the modern world the position of such nobles, both as landowners and administrators, became less important. Many of their privileges disappeared at the time of the French Revolution. The titles and documents of others were destroyed by a rising in the late eighteenth century called in dialect the "burla papai" or "burn the papers." At this time many of them handed over their parchments of their own accord. Three wagonloads of papers were taken away from the castle of Wufflens and burned, to the acute regret of modern historians.

But the peasants in Switzerland did not burn château and nobles, too, as they did in France.

Some of these old families are today impoverished and live very modestly, with only their names to recall past glories. Other old families, adapting themselves to the times, have kept their lands, and still play a part in Swiss life. One branch of a family may be poor, another rich; one cousin may literally be a cow-herd while another lives in a castle. The de Blonays, for example, who were once the powerful rivals of the Counts of Savoy, still own the massive pile above Vevey which bears their name, and another branch of the family possesses the historic castle of Grandson on Lake Neuchâtel and keeps it up with almost feudal splendor. Today lawyers, architects and doctors often bear historic names, and these names have prestige in a land where tradition counts. Their owners may be elected to office, particularly in times of difficulty, or become officers.

The Swiss bourgeoisie, too, has traditions. A Lullin, a Turretini, a Tronchin, a Micheli of Geneva, an Iselin or a Burckhardt of Basel yield to none in pride of race. They feel themselves to be the equals of any titled family in Europe and look on French people who were ennobled by the Empire as far less authentically aristocratic than themselves.

These burgher families ruled Geneva, Basel, Zurich, for centuries, and they were often both skillful and energetic. The possession of burgher rights was the basis of political and social standing. Even today to be "nationalized" in Switzerland a foreigner must obtain the right of bourgeoisie in some Swiss city or village.

The Swiss have a deep sense of the moral significance of life. In their country there are many shrines, among them St. Maurice en Valais, where the Theban Legion was martyred, and where some of the most magnificent religious treasures in Europe are to be found; the great Abbey of Einsiedeln; the Houses of the famous Order of St. Bernard, which is native to Switzerland; and also Calvin's famous Church in Geneva.

No land is more devout than Catholic Switzerland. In its villages the Church is the center of life and the priest the most important person in the community. His influence is so great that the accusation often made against these communities that they are priest-ridden is not wholly without foundation.

Many proofs of the fervor of Swiss faith exist. The little mountain community of Lens, which is very poor according to Swiss standards, some years ago erected a colossal statue of Christ on a rock dominating the village, where it can be seen throughout the surrounding country. The cost of this statue was out of all proportion to the resources of the town, and, sad to say, it is very ugly; yet the people are delightedly proud of it. In the region called Saviez a beautiful old church is the center of several villages. The people of these hamlets have made many sacrifices to repair and keep it up, and recently they equipped it with stained glass windows made by a great artist. The example has been followed by a hundred or more villages, Catholic and Protestant, which have restored their fine old churches.

The Federal Government built a huge dam in the valley of the Dixence at an altitude of 9,000 feet or more, in order to increase Switzerland's water power. Beside the dam, at the foot of the glacier, the workers built a little chapel, very simple but pure in line, of stone taken from the mountain. It is significant to find this shrine of the old faith beside the most recent work of modern engineers.

A Mass in any of the large mountain villages is a remarkable sight. The whole community is there in costume, and often the Mass will be followed by the transaction of public business in the nearby square, for it is the one occasion when all the people assemble. In the season of military service the soldiers who are in the village stand in the aisles and salute with drawn sword or port of arms the reading of the Gospel and the elevation of the Host. No division exists there between Church and State, between spiritual and temporal power. These celebrations give a moving sense of the unity of a whole people.

Religion is equally important in the life of the Protestant cantons. The Swiss National Church and also the so-called "Free" Church, which are both Calvinist, are very much alive. The "Pasteur" is an important figure in most communities. He plays very much the same part that the clergymen of the Church of England have long played in the English countryside. Moreover Protestantism in Switzerland, as in America, has deeply colored the whole thought and philosophy of the nation. It has, by their own admission, influenced the Catholic population, as well as those who do not believe. It is this firm basis of Christian philosophy which makes the Swiss continue to look at life from a moral point of view. It has saved them, to some extent, from the crass materialism of the age and, together with the old tradition of independence, it has armed them against Nazi propaganda. Such a speech as that of Colonel Fry, quoted in Chapter XI, is possible only in a country where spiritual and moral values have continued to be dominant.

On the other hand, the attitude of mind which is loosely called puritanical is very prevalent. The Swiss village of today is much like the New England town of a hundred years ago. Duty is exacting and there is a deep reverence for propriety and decorum. This unconscious puritanism is evident in an instinctive distrust of frivolity, in a parade of simplicity, and a sort of pride in austerity and even in suffering. It is said that in Geneva people mount on stilts to exhibit their mourning! This attitude of mind is particularly evident in French Switzerland. There people feel that it is dangerous, perhaps even immoral, to be too happy or too fortunate. Pleasure is light-minded and enjoyment of this world's goods has an odor of brimstone.

A certain amount of hypocrisy accompanies this puritanism, as it undoubtedly did in New England. People do not always live up to the principles which they profess, and the Swiss in this respect are like others. They continue, however, to respect the principles of morality even when in practice they disregard them. Those who break the moral law must be careful not to be found out. All this is familiar to Americans, and in fact, Anglo-Saxons feel at home in Switzerland more readily than in Latin countries, for the taboos are the same. It must be added that puritanism is largely a middle-class phenomenon. The peasant who lives near to nature is no prude, and his rigid morality is tempered by sound common sense.

With the development of great cities and the growth of large-scale industry the American point of view has changed much during the last forty years. In Switzerland this has been less the case. Life there is simpler and more intimate. It is more highly organized in the human domain, although—or perhaps because—it is less highly developed in the mechanical and physical plane. Religion and the family are still vital influences. Divorce, though growing in frequency, is not so widespread as in America. Men and women still go to church as a rule, both because they want to and because public opinion expects it. There is little cynicism, and the old standards have been to a large extent maintained.

One reason for this is that the Swiss in spite of their taste for travel, and the marked successes which they have won in foreign countries, are not a very mobile people. Those who do not expatriate themselves are apt to remain attached to one spot, one community.

Provincialism can be stuffy, and a jealous fear of superiority, a tendency to petty judgments, are the defects of small communities. These undoubtedly exist in Switzerland, but they are mitigated by the international currents which flow through the country, opening wide horizons to the people of its quiet little towns.

The Swiss qualities—hardihood, simplicity, traditionalism, social-mindedness, and a moral outlook—have made a society that is sure of its values and clear as to its aims. It is the existence of these common qualities and aims among people so different in all other respects that makes the Federal State possible.

VI. PROSPERITY OUT OF NEED

Of all the paradoxes that Switzerland incorporates, the most remarkable is the prosperity enjoyed in a land so ill-endowed by nature. The casual tourist, crossing the country and seeing rocks and glaciers, narrow gorges and dark forests, with villages precariously perched on steep and arid slopes, thinks of it as a splendid wilderness; and he is not wholly mistaken, for the land is poor.

The area of Switzerland (15,940 square miles) is only about one-half that of the State of Maine (33,040 square miles). Nearly a quarter (22.6 per cent) is unfit for cultivation or for human habitation. In spite of this it is densely populated, with a hundred inhabitants per square mile. It has, moreover, none of the natural resources—coal, oil, precious metals and so on —which are crucial in a modern industrial society. Its arable land is severely limited both in quantity and quality. It has no overseas empire, no colonies as have other small countries like Holland, Belgium, and Portugal, to supply it with raw materials and to absorb its manufactured products on preferential terms. It has, finally, no seacoast, with the possibility of trade and commerce which that advantage implies. It is physically a small, poor, land-locked country.

Yet Switzerland enjoys a standard of living far higher than those of many nations richer in natural resources such as Hungary, Rumania, or Italy. Not only is the average Swiss income relatively high, but it is evenly distributed and, as we have seen, a great deal of comfort and well-being are to be found in most Swiss homes. One need not be a materialist to see that this fact is of vital importance in judging the success of the Federal State.

Swiss prosperity is an absolute rebuttal of the current assumption that the one basis for a thriving industry and national wealth is the possession of physical resources. This idea lies behind the German claim for "living room," that is to say, political domination over the lands which supply them with raw materials. The Swiss have never controlled their markets nor their sources of raw materials, yet they have built up one of the most successful industrial structures of our era.

Switzerland is not merely a land of mountaintops and rural villages. Almost a half of its working population (forty-six per cent) is engaged in one form or another of manufacture. Less than thirty per cent live by agriculture. The remaining fifth work in hotels, in transport, in the professions and in the administration. On the whole, then, the Swiss economy is surprisingly industrialized.

The most important single fact about the economic working of Switzerland is that her foreign trade per capita is higher than that of any other industrialized country in the world. It has been calculated that seventy francs' worth of goods are exported every year per inhabitant. This is an extraordinary achievement for a country with limited natural resources and with a relatively large agricultural population.

How has this paradox of prosperity in a land that is naturally poor been achieved? It is often assumed today that centralization is a great economic advantage to every nation; that only a strong Government with wide powers of coordination and coercion can secure efficiency, well-being, and a high level of prosperity. Decentralization, it is said, weakens the national economy, lowers efficiency, and places the country at a grave disadvantage in dealing with other nations where state control is more advanced. Switzerland absolutely contradicts this premise.

Economic liberalism, at least since the publication of Adam Smith's *Wealth of Nations,* has carried with it certain specific, almost technical connotations; it has meant relatively free competition internally, relatively free trade with foreign nations; it has called for a concentration on those pursuits for which a country was best fitted by its natural advantages, and for a maximum of ingenuity and efficiency in the development of such advantages. In recent times the precepts of economic liberalism have been expanded to admit a measure of government intervention or co-operative enterprise in cases where private initiative fails to act, or acts in a manner detrimental to the public interest. Examples of this in modern Switzerland are laws designed to achieve social security and to prevent the destruction of timber resources.

Both the structure and the institutions of the Swiss economy conform to liberalism thus defined. The Swiss have not had the illusion that they could profitably be self-sufficient. They have regarded themselves as part of a world economy, and their high standard of living attests the benefits they have derived from this outlook. In the present era their commercial and industrial success has been won by a high degree of specialization and by the almost miserly exploitation of every natural advantage.

In agriculture, for example, the Swiss did not attempt fully to supply their own food requirements. They made a virtue of necessity. More than a third of the productive land has been turned over to cattle-raising. Grain, fruit, and vegetables are imported on a considerable scale while the uniquely Swiss agricultural products—cheese, condensed milk and chocolate—are exported. Each of these commodities represents a more or less refined stage of manufacture. It is typical of the Swiss economy that its agricultural resources are worked to their most advanced point before they are sent abroad.

The Swiss are not, of course, completely dependent

on foods imported from abroad; only a quarter of their foreign imports are foodstuffs. It is rather that they have preferred, when international conditions permitted, to trade their way to a higher standard of living. This they could do because of the highly specialized character of their products. But in times of war, when international markets were cut off, Switzerland has been able, largely, to feed herself. Even then her particular wares have been of use to her. From 1914 to 1918 she was able to exchange chocolate and cheese with her neighbors in return for the coal and wheat she needed.

The tendency fully to exploit domestic manufacturing skills is evident throughout Swiss industry. Except for an abundant supply of potential waterpower Switzerland contains virtually no physical resources on which a national industrial structure could be erected. The mineral riches of the land are confined to a little salt, some iron ore, and manganese. Yet the Swiss are, as we have pointed out, a manufacturing nation.

We saw that only about a quarter of the total Swiss imports are foodstuffs; the remainder is made up equally of raw materials and manufactured goods. Fully three-fifths of the articles entering the country are in a crude state. These imports are paid for by a variety of exports (supplemented by some tourist trade), almost all of which, including agricultural products, are in a manufactured or semi-manufactured state. Raw materials represent only seven per cent of Switzerland's export trade, foodstuffs six per cent and manufactured goods eighty-seven per cent. That is to say, roughly ninety per cent of those products which are sent abroad have been increased in value by Swiss ingenuity and craftsmanship.

In 1937, for example, exports may be broken down as follows (in per cent of total value):

Watches (including parts)	18.8%
Machinery, instruments, etc.	18.2
Textiles (principally silks and cottons)	18.2
Chemicals and drugs	7.0
Dyes, colors, paints	6.9
Metals (raw and semi-manufactured)	6.5
Metals (manufactured)	5.3
Foods and drinks	5.7
Miscellaneous	13.4
	100.0%

It is obvious from this table how large a proportion of Swiss exports are goods whose production demands advanced skills. Watches, electrical machinery, engines of various types, embroidered and woven goods, form more than fifty-five per cent of them.

In order to win and keep their place in the world market the Swiss have relied to some extent on their central position in Europe, which gives their goods easy rail access to Austria, France, Germany, and Italy. This has, in some degree, compensated for the lack of seacoast. But they have depended primarily upon the quality of their production. In this they have been aided by the possession of many highly skilled workers, and the peculiar combination, in many domains, of individual effort with co-operation.

In agriculture the use of all available resources is particularly striking. The highest vineyards and the highest wheat fields in the world are in Switzerland. Tourists who travel in the canton of the Valais, in the Bernese Oberland, the Grisons, or in any of the Swiss mountain districts are always astonished to see villages perched on the mountainside at apparently inaccessible heights, barns and lofts built among the rocks. The pastures run often to the very foot of the glaciers. No inch of ground is lost, and the sure-footed cattle wander in uplands which from the valley look unbelievably steep and remote.

In the lake regions the vineyards are a great source of wealth, and it is the steep and sun-baked slopes which yield the best grapes. These slopes have been carefully terraced so as to lose no inch of precious soil, and they have been buttressed against the torrential rains. Around Lake Leman they run down to the very edge of the water and up to the rim of the forest, where vines will no longer grow. The enormous labor required to develop these terraced vineyards was undertaken long ago by the monks. The names of the Valaisan wines still recall their ancient origin: Amigne was once "vinum amoenum," Umagne was "vinum humanum," and the Heide Wein was the wine of the pagans. The labor of keeping up terraces and buttressed slopes is endless. A storm which brings down stones and earth from above may necessitate months of repair work. Forest conservation has also been developed to a high point in Switzerland, and Swiss foresters are famous in Europe. The most remote sections of the mountain ranges are watched over carefully, and wasteful deforestation is unknown.

A striking example of the Swiss capacity for using every asset is their tourist trade. It was the "mad English travelers" who taught them in the eighteenth century the commercial value of their mountains and lakes. A network of roads, of hotels, and later of funicular railways grew up all over the country. The Swiss love of order and cleanliness, their gift for organization makes them such excellent hotel-keepers that a number of the best hotels all over the world, including all the Ritz establishments, are owned and run by Swiss. There are several important schools for hotel-keepers in Switzerland whose diplomas are internationally respected.

The tourist trade is not, as foreigners are apt to imagine, the most important Swiss industry; yet it did bring a considerable sum of money into the country every year, and it gave employment to a considerable number of people. The funds it drew were, moreover, foreign exchange and thus directly applicable to the purchase of the imports upon which the nation thrived.

After the first World War, however, life in Switzerland became relatively expensive because the Swiss franc was not devalued to the level of other currencies. Other regions—the Riviera, the Dalmatian Coast, the Austrian Tyrol—began to attract the wandering Britain or American. The Swiss hotels never fully recovered their prosperity. Efforts were made to keep the tourist industry alive in the hope of an eventual return of the foreign clientèle. Hotels were often kept open at a loss and prices were cut to the bone. Yet the tourist trade failed to revive and the world depression accentuated its decline after 1929.

Swiss schools have also had a large foreign following. People sent their children to them to learn French or German and to profit by the outdoor life which these institutions offered. The quality of Swiss education attracted parents in England, Holland, and the Scandinavian countries as well as in America. Here, too, post-war conditions affected Switzerland unfavorably.

Perhaps the most important example of Switzerland's determination to use all its resources has been the development of waterpower. Few countries are richer in this, for the head-waters of many rivers are in its mountain ranges; and its high-lying lakes can be dammed so as to give an enormous fall. The exploitation of "white-coal" began early, but it was speeded up by the experience of 1914-1918. The greatest hardship of Switzerland during the first World War was the lack of coal. Having almost no supply of its own, it was obliged to bargain with its neighbors for the quantity absolutely necessary for its railroads, factories, and homes. Determined that this should not happen again, it began after 1918 to develop to a much higher point its electrical resources. Nearly all its railroads and by far the greater part of its industries are now electrified. Vast new dams have been built in recent years so that by 1939 Switzerland was able to sell power to its neighbors as well as to make the fullest use of it at home.

Switzerland has cultivated intensely not only its pasturage, vineyards, forests, and waterpower, but also the skills of its working population. In agriculture itself, in dairy work, in the culture of the grape and the making of wine, the Swiss are experienced and have developed great technical skill. So much is this the case in regard to wine that as early as the eighteenth century when Catherine the Great of Russia wanted to establish vineyards in Bessarabia she sent for peasants from the canton of Vaud to teach the people of her country their methods. A colony of Vaudois still exists in that remote province. Swiss viticulturists have been very successful in Algeria also, and in the United States.

In industry, hereditary skills have been of importance. We have seen that the watch-making industry leads in the list of Swiss exports. This is because nowhere else in the world can a comparable group of skilled artisans for this delicate trade be found. The Swiss worker virtually defies competition. Even in America and in France those who make or repair high-grade watches are almost always Swiss. The makers of the finest watchsprings earn as much as ten or even twenty dollars a day at their trade—an enormous sum for Switzerland—and they could not easily be replaced, for it requires early training and long experience to acquire the necessary fineness of touch and precision of movement.

In the making of electrical machinery, turbines, generators, cables, meters, and so on, Switzerland has excelled largely because of the quality of its labor. It enjoys, as well, a reputation for the quality of its steam and internal combustion engines, Diesel motors, pumps, mills, and all kinds of scientific instruments and instruments of precision, and these specialized industries also require highly skilled labor.

Various forms of co-operation, many with a long tradition, play a role in Switzerland equivalent to centralized planning in other nations. A large part of the agricultural population of Switzerland lives in hamlets or villages. Each of these is a more or less independent entity, whose prosperity does not come from the neighboring cities nor from passersby, but rather from its own appanage of fields, vineyards, or high pasture lands and alps. The economic aspects of communal life in these mountain districts are particularly interesting.

The grazing lands, or "alps," are in large part the property of the village. These pastures often lie at a great distance from the community to which they belong, and they are usually at different altitudes, the lower ones, called "mayens," being used in the spring, and other higher ones in midsummer. To these various pastures the village herds are driven in April or May. Every inhabitant of the village has the right to send his cows with the common herd and the herdsman is chosen and paid by the community. He spends the whole summer on the alps, moving his herd according to the state of the weather and the pasturage, and making on the spot the cheeses which are a large part of the wealth of the community. These cheeses belong to the village as a whole. They are sold in due season and the produce is divided among the villagers in proportion to the number and quality of cows that they have had in the herd. It is impossible to buy a cheese from the cow-herd upon the alp, as tourists sometimes discover. He cannot sell them because they do not belong to him. He is responsible for them to the village whose employee he is.

Many of the lower pasture lands and often the villages themselves depend on glacial water brought down from the high regions in irrigating ditches which are called "bisses." These ditches are often very old. Some of them, in fact, date back to the fourteenth and fifteenth centuries. They were originally built by the peasants of the community and in many cases they still belong to the descendants of those who made them. Ownership in the bisse goes with ownership of the land.

Built to bring the water down as directly as possible to the fields and pastures with the least possible loss on the way, a bisse often runs right against the face of the mountain. It is supported on iron stakes driven into the rocks, so that it hangs over a precipice two thousand feet deep with a wall two thousand feet high above. It is made of planks, and a narrow path runs beside the box which carries the water. The bisse must be kept up and repaired, and the responsibility for doing so rests with the owners of the lands which it waters. A share in the ditch brings the right to so many hours of water per week, but also the obligation of helping to keep it up. Every year in the spring when the planks are slippery a few men fall from these vertiginous aerial paths and as one walks along the bisse one sees from time to time a cross cut in the wall of rock. Here someone fell—pray for his soul! These ditches, held in common for centuries by the members of a community, are characteristic products of the Swiss combination of individualism and co-operative enterprise.

Another aspect of village co-operation is the institution of the public baker. Bread is the staple article of diet. The oven usually belongs to the whole village, and the bread is baked once a week or sometimes once a month for the community. The baker is almost a political personage. In some villages he is elected for a year or for a period of months.

In the villages of the lower regions co-operation has been of particular value in the cheese and wine industries. Quality is important to both of these products. Standardized production for commercial purposes tends, as a rule, to lower quality, but with both wine and cheese, local conditions, such as weather or soil, may cause great variation in the product from place to place and from year to year. The dairy and wine co-operatives of Switzerland have improved rather than lowered the quality of the goods, especially in districts where this was second-rate. The finest wines of Vaud, or the Valais or Neuchâtel, are still privately owned, and so, too, are the best cheeses of Gruyère, but the co-operatives have helped production in less-favored regions.

For instance, in the wine-growing district known as "La Côte" which lies between Lausanne and Geneva, the wine is of second-rate quality, and in years when there is little sun it is very acid.[1] There are some better vineyards in the region, however, and a good year will give wine that is acceptable. The viticultural co-

[1] It is said that in Gualion, where grow the highest vineyards of the canton of Vaud, that when the time comes to vintage the mayor puts a bunch of grapes under his saddle and rides around the town. If the grapes have run they vintage at once, but if the grapes are hard and still intact they wait a week to make the wine.

operatives mix the wines from the various vineyards so as to give an average blend and they will hold the wine of bad years over to mix it with that of better ones. Few peasants could afford to keep their vintage from year to year in this way. The co-operatives bottle the wine in standard form and advertise it so that it may find a market wider than the local one. Moreover both in Vaud and Valais the co-operatives have made possible the use of modern machinery, such as hydraulic wine presses, which enormously decrease the labor of the vintage, but which are far beyond the means of the individual wine growers.

The cheese-making co-operatives have given the peasants a stable market for his milk. They have to some extent standardized Swiss cheese, but not entirely to the disadvantage of the public, for they have been strong enough to fight against the competition of poorer products from the French Jura and to protect the title of "Switzerland Cheese." This is the only genuine article and it is made in some three thousand *Käsereien,* many of them quite small. It is gathered, tested, and marketed abroad by the powerful co-operative association whose advertisements are familiar to American readers. Here the work of a resourceful and well-organized co-operative has enabled the Swiss product to compete with the cheap imitations produced by Dutch, German, Scandinavian, and even pirate Swiss cheeses. A curious result of the cheese co-operatives is that in Switzerland, the land of cows, it is difficult to get cream or milk in small quantities. Almost all goes to the co-operatives.

Yet the co-operatives in Switzerland have not taken on the importance they had in Denmark. They have improved the economic life of the peasant by allowing the use of modern methods and modern machinery. They have helped him to market his products, but this problem was not acute, for Switzerland consumes a large part of her own wines and a goodly proportion of her own cheeses. Swiss co-operatives have not, therefore, become a sort of autonomous power, a state within the state, as seems to have been to some extent the case in the Scandinavian countries. In Switzerland co-operation is a method of production, not a solution of the social problem.

That the general standard of living in Switzerland is high is due also to the relatively wide and even distribution of wealth. Swiss farms and landholdings are on the average small. The country does not lend itself to vast estates. The scale and technique of Swiss farming bear a close resemblance to those used in neighboring France and Southern Germany. The same variety of culture, the same relative self-sufficiency, exist. On most farms pigs and chickens, vegetables, a crop of potatoes, hops, or a small vineyard, and often a few beehives supplement the main crop.

There is great independence in the life of the Swiss land-owning peasant. Unlike the American farmer, he looks on the land as a way of life, not as a business.

Food, lodging, security for himself and his family, are the greater part of what he expects to get from his farm. He uses much of what he raises himself, and sells the surplus, a calf or two, a few pigs and chickens, eggs, butter, or vegetables, in a nearby market. The well-to-do peasant kills his own pigs, smokes his hams, prepares his sausages. He makes his own wine or beer, and these are usually of excellent quality, often far better than that served in the hotels.

Such holdings are rather like the subsistence farms which have been talked of occasionally in America as a solution for unemployment. Garden and dove-cote, beehive and orchard, help to enrich life. They are sometimes almost as lucrative as the wheat fields or the pasture. There are many kinds of labor and of yield which complete and sustain each other, forming a sort of rustic cycle, so that for the peasant no year is wholly bad, and life, though it follows a regular pattern, is not monotonous.

The existence of local markets is an important factor in the economic life of the Swiss countryside. In every town some particular square or street is given over at least once a week to the market. There the women of the countryside come to sell their butter and eggs, their surplus vegetables, their chickens, their honey, and sometimes flowers from their gardens and mushrooms from the nearby woods. In the meantime, the men will dispose of a pig, a calf, or a cow and negotiate the sale of the wheat or the wine for the year. This enables the country people to escape the tyranny of the middleman. They can sell their surplus from week to week and do not have to pack their produce for the city market.

Obviously these methods, though primitive in the eyes of the American business farmer, help the rural community to be self-sufficient. Only a generation ago, an eccentric Swiss landowner boasted that he could raise all he needed on his own estate. In addition to food and wine, he grew flax, kept a few sheep for wool, cultivated silkworms on his mulberry trees and raised a little tobacco and some beets for sugar. He burned the wood from his own forest and even went so far as to use home-made tallow candles or colza oil to light his house. Tea, coffee, and salt were all that he absolutely had to buy. Of course, this assertion of economic independence was expensive and artificial. It is true, however, that a peasant farm may be to a large extent a self-sufficient unit.

There is, of course, some poverty in the industrial cities of Switzerland, and the usual problems of the liberal state, unemployment and labor disputes, have arisen. They have not, however, been as troublesome as in most other industrial countries. One reason for this is that until recent years the connection between the urban and the rural populations was very close. Even today a number of Swiss industries are located in small communities, where the workers can have gardens or even small farms or vineyards, and so be in a measure agriculturists as well as factory hands. This combination of rural and industrial life makes for contentment and stability.

Swiss manufacturing plants are, for the most part, small units employing trained workers, although there are some notable exceptions. The goods made in these factories must be marketed abroad, and this, as a keen critic of Switzerland has pointed out, fosters a kind of "conservative cosmopolitanism" even among the workers, and tends to make them as eager for industrial peace at home as for international peace abroad.

The relative liberalism of the nineteenth century was very favorable to Swiss economy, and until 1914 the country enjoyed an expanding national wealth. The first world war put a great strain upon Switzerland's resources, yet, on the other hand, neutrality had some advantages. Switzerland was able to sell its goods to all its warring neighbors. There was a boom in certain branches of Swiss industry, just as there was in America. This boom, however, was short-lived. After the war many mushroom industries failed, and there were years of depression and readjustment.

The period between the two European wars saw a steady world-wide growth of economic nationalism. A shop in Geneva displayed each year a large map of Europe where the frontiers were marked by walls whose height was in proportion to the tariff barriers erected by each nation. Every year the walls grew higher and higher, until they almost hid the countries themselves. The map was truly symbolic. Each country was determined to export a maximum and import a minimum of goods. Obviously such a state of things was peculiarly unfavorable to Switzerland, yet Swiss industry managed to survive, and Swiss statesmen pursued a classic liberal policy to the last ditch.

The inherent conservatism of the people and their leaders was never more clearly illustrated than during the years that followed upon 1929. Switzerland shared the sharp decline in world trade that then occurred. In 1931, however, when Britain went off the gold standard Switzerland did not follow, but chose to join the so-called gold bloc: France, Holland, Belgium, and Switzerland.

This tight-lipped gesture meant that the Swiss currency was expensive for tourists and that Swiss goods were abnormally dear in the international market. The hotel trade, which supplied part of the foreign exchange with which to purchase immediate imports, was badly hit, and imports fell off, despite a considerable sacrifice of Swiss gold and securities held abroad.

The extent of the decline in foreign trade, prices, and employment from 1929 to 1932 are indicated by the following figures:

	1929	*1932*
Imports (million francs)	228	147
Exports (million francs)	175	67
Wholesale prices	100	68
Unemployment (%)	1.8	10.8

What lay behind this policy was a deep-seated mistrust of the kind of currency manipulation then in vogue. It was associated in the Swiss mind with inflation. Depreciation of the currency would have meant some rise in domestic prices, and those who lived on fixed incomes would have suffered. It would have meant, especially, a decline in value of the widely held Swiss Government bonds. Moreover, experience seemed to show that inflation was only a palliative, not a remedy for the difficulties of international trade. Wisely or not the Swiss chose the hard course. They preserved the traditional integrity of the Swiss franc in the world market; they maintained the purchasing power of the interest of the government debt; but they faced a grueling deflationary force in the form of decreased tourist trade and a poor bargaining position in the markets where Swiss exports were sold.

A special kind of pride also influenced Switzerland's decision not to follow the British into devaluation in 1931. For many centuries the Swiss, lying on the central trading routes of Europe, have served as bankers for the Continent. In modern times Geneva, Basel, and Lausanne carried on this tradition. In the early thirties every political and financial crisis induced a flow of funds to Switzerland from Vienna, Berlin, Paris, and even London. The Swiss were justly proud of the confidence the Continent seemed to place in the franc and wished to justify that confidence. Banking circles, moreover, wielded a considerable influence in the country, and their weight was thrown heavily to the side of financial orthodoxy. In a sense this attitude was quixotic. The whole structure of free trade and free capital movements was crumbling. Switzerland could not, in fact, hold out alone. But to Switzerland's bankers, to her middle classes, and even to the working population currency devaluation represented a kind of public immorality and it was fought to the end. Towards the close of September, 1937, the gold bloc cracked. Its members realized that they had not fully shared the recovery that less orthodox countries had enjoyed in the period of 1932-1936. Their gold holdings were dwindling, interest rates were high, credit tight, unemployment still rising. France led the way in this capitulation, and the smaller nations were forced to follow her in devaluation. The French franc, however, was reduced in value by sixty per cent and the Swiss franc by a mere thirty per cent—the minimum compatible with an even partial adjustment to world forces.

For Switzerland, devaluation was inevitable once France took the step. The French were the second largest purchasers of Swiss goods after Germany, and exports to France would have been critically affected if Switzerland had stood out. Furthermore, 1936 was for the Swiss a very difficult year. In January, unemployment was as high as nineteen per cent of the working population; and the unstable monetary situation had led to a large-scale hoarding of gold and a general reluctance to undertake any type of new enterprise. Even under these circumstances a considerable portion of the population opposed devaluation. Action was postponed by the government until the last minute, and the opposition almost succeeded in unseating the President of the Council.

The fear of inflation which was largely back of this opposition proved unfounded. The Swiss devaluation was handled with great skill, and it inflicted a minimum of suffering. Action was immediately taken to prevent a speculative rise in prices and custom duties, and import quotas were lowered in order to insure a plentiful supply of cheap goods. Between 1936 and the outbreak of war in 1939 the rise in Swiss prices was unimportant. Unemployment, moreover, fell steadily, and although export markets and the tourist trade were not fully regained, Switzerland seemed to have emerged with fair success from the crisis.

The extent of the recovery from 1932 to 1939 is indicated by the following figures:

	1932	*1939*
Imports (million francs)	147	157
Exports (million francs)	67	108
Wholesale prices	68	70

Unemployment had fallen to about five per cent by the close of 1938.

The financial story of Switzerland in the nineteen thirties, and in fact her whole recent economic history, is consistent with her historic development. In the liberal economic tradition of the nineteenth century the Swiss found a framework ideal for their special organization. The compromise between international co-operation and a federalized nationalism offered by that framework exactly suited the temper and structure of Swiss life. The nation was loath to abandon the forms which once represented the central vitality of the nineteenth-century world.

The lesson of Swiss economy is plain. Neither natural resources nor empire are the true sources of national prosperity and individual well-being. In the face of this established fact the contention of imperialists all over the world that their territorial greeds are motivated by a desire for a higher standard of living for their own people seems singularly hollow.

Swiss economic history proves that a state whose policy is liberal both internally and in the international field may enjoy a prosperity as great as any to be had by nationalistic or totalitarian means. But Switzerland's well-being and even its survival do depend on the existence of some degree of economic freedom and rational exchange among the nations. In the economic, as in the political field, danger for Switzerland comes from the selfishness of nations that are not willing to earn their way to prosperity by hard work and the use of what resources they have, but which prefer to snatch by force of arms the advantages they desire.

What the Swiss hope from a reconstituted Europe is a return of the paradox of their pre-war life. They want a maximum of international exchange of goods, a minimum of direct political and cultural interference from the outside. They must send their watches, machinery, lace, and cheeses over the continent. They must receive raw and semi-manufactured goods from the world outside. Borders must be opened for the tourist. Their modern history indicates that this ideal is not impossible of fulfillment. It is power politics, not genuine economic realities, that makes it difficult to attain.

The Swiss have more than once adapted their social and economic structure to changing circumstances. They lived successfully in the midst of the feudal states of the late Middle Ages and with the great mercantilist empires. In a federated Europe, trade agreements made under the auspices of a continent-wide organization might be as favorable to them as the status of 1914. They are not, however, prepared to accept conditions that involve the sacrifice of their political independence. They wish for no new order, however profitable, under German hegemony. They have thus far placed their federal integrity above economic advantage, and they will unquestionably continue to do so.

VII. CULTURE

A COUNTRY which has four languages cannot have a homogeneous culture, and if three of these languages belong to great neighboring civilizations, its culture cannot be entirely autonomous. Yet Switzerland has given its artistic and intellectual creations depth and originality, and in certain fields it has produced a remarkable synthesis of Latin and Germanic virtues.

In order to discuss Swiss culture we would have to find something in common between such different spirits as Zwingli, Paracelsus, Euler, Pestalozzi, J. J. Rousseau, Madame de Staël, Gottfried Keller, H. F. Amiel, Karl Barth, C. F. Ramuz, C. G. Jung, to mention only the universally known men of genius that Switzerland has produced. Can this be done?

Three primary facts must be kept in mind: Switzerland is a *small* federal democracy; it is a stark, upland country; it is a crossroads. These facts eliminate many possibilities which exist elsewhere, but they create others which are to be found in Switzerland alone. The general aspects of "Swiss" culture are thus to a large extent predetermined by the physical and political structure of the country.

In this little federal democracy cultural life was never centralized by a court or a capital. The history of ideas in Switzerland could not be described by generations nor by schools, as it is in France. It is the history of a series of cultural centers which have arisen, shone, and died out here and there, simultaneously or successively, according to language, religion, or political and economic vicissitudes. In the Middle Ages the monasteries of German Switzerland—St. Gall, where Notker Le Begue composed his celebrated Gregorian sequences in the ninth century; Thurgovia, where Germanic mysticism flourished, and later Einsiedeln, of which Zwingli was the abbot—were centers with a European reputation.

In the sixteenth century Basel and Geneva suddenly took on world importance. With Erasmus, Holbein, and the first great printers, Basel became one of the pillars of the humanistic Renaissance. With Calvin and Theodore Beza, Geneva became the fortress of theological reaction against the Renaissance. Zurich had its turn in the eighteenth century. Center of the "Swiss school," it exercised for several decades a sort of hegemony over German literary life. At the same time French Switzerland became the refuge of those who were in opposition to the absolutist régime in France; Voltaire established his headquarters there, flooded Europe with letters and pamphlets and quarreled with the Consistory of the Clergy of Geneva to whom Rousseau had just submitted. In Napoleon's day all the French Intelligentsia migrated to the shores of Lake Leman. A second "Swiss school," romantic and liberal, was born in the château of Coppet under the auspices of Madame de Staël, daughter of the Genevese banker, Necker, who was the last minister of Louis XVI. This circle disappeared with the Restoration. Another one, more austere and theological, soon grew up in Lausanne where the gentle Vinet tried to convert Sainte-Beuve. Another was founded in Basel around the great historian, Jakob Burckhardt, and his young admirer, Nietzsche; around Bachofen, the theorist of matriarchy; around the skeptical theologian Overbeck. After the peace of 1919 the splendid early days of the League of Nations revived, for a few years, by its publications, its salons, its international institutions, the influence of Coppet. Zurich became after 1933 the rendezvous of writers exiled by Fascism or Hitlerism, and Basel is today the citadel of the dialectical theologians of the school of Karl Barth, driven out of the German universities.

Obviously each of these centers was created by the conjunction of international spirits with a small milieu having strong local traditions. Switzerland was not merely a sort of hotel for the French, Italians, Germans, and Englishmen who found there a temporary asylum; all these men mixed with the society of the city which welcomed them, and they made friends with its best minds. They acted, thought, created and learned to live in a framework and among customs which were wholly republican. Their works show obvious signs of it. Through them Switzerland became a school of western democracy. For centuries she played the part in Europe which the United States, refuge of the exiles of totalitarianism, seems called upon to play in the world of today and tomorrow.

Political federalism implies diverse centers of culture. Moreover in a small democracy—perhaps in any democracy worthy of the name—there must exist a vigorous taste for education, a preoccupation with it.

We have seen that the Swiss is didactic, that he has both the gift and the passion for education. This characteristic is to be found not only among Swiss theologians, moralists and psychologists, but even in the best poets and novelists. Rousseau preached perpetually in all his books; Albert de Haller, the greatest man Berne produced during the aristocratic period, is best known for a long didactic poem on the Alps; Jeremia Gotthelf, who was a country clergyman in the nineteenth century, produced a considerable body of novels which are among the finest works of German literature but which are nothing but a vast sermon splendidly illustrated. Even in *Green Henry,* that masterpiece by Gottfried Keller, the progressive radical of Zurich, there are to be found, side by side with the moving lyrical passages, a quantity of didactic reflections which draw a moral even from the most fantastic and romantic events.

Thus it is not astonishing that Switzerland gave birth to the greatest pedagogue of modern times: Pestalozzi; to his Catholic disciple, Father Girard; and to Rousseau, who in *Emile* showed himself a realistic and competent precursor of modern educational methods. Even today Switzerland is at the forefront of the educational movement and it is perhaps in this domain that it has shown most daring and most creative imagination. The Rousseau Institute in Geneva, directed by well-known psychologists such as Pierre Bovet, Jean Piaget, and Edouard Claparede, has developed educators from all countries. Its guiding idea is typically Swiss and even federalist; it is to waken in each individual both a personal initiative and the idea of social service. It is to wish man to be "master of himself in order that he may serve others," according to Vinet's maxim.

A rude land where men live close to each other, but also a land of altitude, where glacial sublimity and daily prose are in close contact: this is the second factor which determines the character of Swiss culture. The material and social conditions of the country have created in the Swiss a remarkable gift of craftsmanship, a genius for taking advantage of everything, for wasting nothing and adjusting and ordering all things to the highest point. Outwardly the country itself affords the spectacle of a well-made machine, very complex, but beautifully polished and kept up with scrupulous care. This practical sense, this feeling for economy, this imagination turned towards the knowledge and improvement of reality rather than towards pure speculation are facts which explain why the Swiss have a scientific rather than a poetic spirit. When a Swiss has a great vision, he does not write an eloquent speech nor a passionate poem; he makes a huge bridge—like the Washington Bridge which was built by the Swiss engineer Ammann, or the longest tunnel in Europe, like the Simplon.

Of the seven Nobel prizes which have been awarded to Swiss citizens in these last decades only one went to a poet—Carl Spitteler. The others were given to chemists, doctors, naturalists, or mathematicians. The proportion is significant. In all the centuries cities like Basel and Geneva did not produce a single poet worthy of the name, whereas among their aristocracy real scientific dynasties developed, such as the de Saussures and the Forels in the domain of natural sciences, the Bernouilli and the Burckhardts of Basel in mathematics and history. Neuchâtel, a little city of 23,000 inhabitants, has not yet found its writer, but it has given birth to Emer de Vattel, one of the founders of international law, to Osterwald, theologian and translator of the Bible, and to the Agassiz family whose brilliant career America has witnessed.

For the birth and development of a great poet

more "play" is necessary—more waste of time and thought, more leisure, solitude and spiritual vagabondage than Switzerland can give or tolerate. It should be added that scientific work, which is essentially collective or co-operative, corresponds to the temper of the country. The Swiss scientist is not merely the man of the laboratory—it is rare that we find him isolating himself in his specialties. In general he is remarkably human, he has a great part in the social, civic, and even religious life of his canton. Thus Leonard Euler, one of the greatest mathematicians of the modern era, spent a large part of his time in defending and illustrating the Christian faith, as his correspondence shows. But if Swiss poetic genius in the broadest sense has found expression rarely and incompletely in poems, it has found compensation in unexpected domains. In this land without plains, cut up into pigeon holes, the imagination can move freely only towards the heights and the depths—whether physically, in looking at the Alps, or symbolically in the regions of the spirit. Moreover this imagination, however far it may go in daring, never ceases to aim at a sort of superior utility. It was not for the sake of fame or sport that the Vaudois Professor, Piccard, went up into stratosphere, but to bring down information as to those regions. Why is it that when he wants to rise into spiritual heights the Swiss thinker chooses a theological rather than a speculative path? For a single relatively important speculative philosopher, Charles Secretan (nineteenth century), the country has given, from the time of Zwingli to that of Karl Barth, passing through Pierre Viret, Turretini, Osterwald, Frederick Godet, Alexander Vinet, Emil Brunner, a pleiad of theologians of first rank. This is because theology seeks to act concretely, whereas philosophy describes and proposes its truths abstractly. In the same way if a Swiss philosopher explores the depths of the soul it is again with the object of drawing from his most daring speculations some applicable conclusions. Paracelsus in the sixteenth century and C. G. Jung in our own day, who may be considered as sorcerers or magi, are poets—the one of the occult, the other of the subconscious. But they are also practitioners, doctors, givers of moral advice and formulae, who never lose sight of the total humanity for which they labor.

Switzerland is not only a small and mountainous country, but also a land of passes. We have seen that it was born of the fertilization of a privileged local situation by the communal ideas which came across the Gothard. To the primitive cell of the forest cantons other cantons of different tongues and religions were added, so that the movement of European ideas became richer and more rapid. Of course, the famous refugees whom Switzerland housed through the whole course of its history contributed generously to this development. Erasmus came from Rotterdam,

Calvin from Picardy, Voltaire and Joseph de Maistre mingled in the intellectual life of Geneva and Lausanne. The young Nietzsche, appointed to a professor's chair in Basel, went to spend his weekends with Richard and Cosima Wagner, who lived on an island near Lucerne. The war of 1914 brought Lenin, Romain Rolland, and their revolutionary or pacifist disciples to Switzerland. It brought also the Polish writer and patriot Sienkiewicz, and the Russian musician Stravinsky. Soon after, Rainer Maria Rilke came to live in his tower of Musot in the Valais. The totalitarian persecution exiled to the banks of the lakes of Zurich, Locarno and Geneva, Thomas Mann, Emil Ludwig, Guglielmo Ferrero, Ignazio Silone, and other celebrities of whom a large number have since emigrated to America.

But Switzerland has for its part always sent its greatest spirits abroad; they have needed a wider field of experience and a larger public. They have often played a considerable part in their land of adoption, and almost always they have ended by returning to their own country to enrich it with a new glory. This transposition into a spiritual plane of the idea of the "foreign service," this exportation of men and ideas balances the importation of the refugees. Many of the greatest Swiss citizens have made their names far from their own country—Rousseau and Benjamin Constant in France, Lavater and Gottfried Keller in Germany. In the twentieth century it has come to be almost a rule that a Swiss writer or artist can reach fame and make his reputation only in a foreign capital. The best Swiss authors are published in Paris, in Milan, or in Berlin. They have almost all of them spent a part of their lives in one or another of these capitals, and it has often happened that they are better known there than in their own canton.

A witty citizen of Geneva, writer of the last century, Marc Monnier, summed up this fecund exchange in a brief talk given before his Paris colleagues. "Messieurs les Français," he said, "you gave us Calvin, we sent you Rousseau. Let us begin again."

Because of this constant exchange, the Swiss intellectual has become a man given to comparison, a kind of necessary middle-man of culture, a translator in the widest sense of the word. It was a citizen of Berne, Bear de Muralt, whose *Letters on the French and English,* published at the beginning of the eighteenth century, aroused an interest in England and English affairs on the continent. It was Madame de Staël and Benjamin Constant who revealed the wealth of German thought—Goethe, Schiller and the romantic philosophers—to the post-Napoleonic generation. Charles Maurras, the royalist philosopher and pamphleteer, has frequently inveighed against the little court which gathered around Madame de Staël at Coppet as being at the bottom of all that he hated in republican France, for it was actually through that famous "gap of Coppet," between the Lake and the Jura, that liberal ideas entered the Latin world. It was two Swiss historians, Philippe Monnier and Jakob Burckhardt, who revived knowledge and appreciation of the Italian Renaissance in the nineteenth century, the first by a charming "Quatro-cento," the second by a monumental work on the spirit of the Renaissance which greatly influenced Nietzsche and through him touched a large part of contemporary thought.

It should astonish no one to find that France discovered foreign contemporary literatures through the intermediary of Swiss critics and Swiss magazines. We will mention here among many possible names only those of Maurice Muret, whose books on Germany and Italy were considered authoritative even before 1914, and of Robert de Traz, the founder of the *Revue de Genève,* which after the peace of 1919 reflected the spirit of the early days of the League of Nations. To it most of the political men of the day contributed, and in its pages were first published in translation the works of Thomas Mann, D. H. Lawrence, Katherine Mansfield, Ortega y Gasset, Sherwood Anderson, Virginia Woolf, Keyserling, and Pirandello.

What we have said heretofore may give the impression that Swiss culture tends to create high averages rather than exceptional individuals. That is true. But whereas this kind of fundamental though unformulated law of Swiss democracy has no exception on the civic level (the great art of the Swiss political man is to *efface* himself), it is remarkable that in the domain of culture powerful personalities have succeeded in reaching full development. It is true that often they have been recognized and adopted by their compatriots only after they have made their mark on wider stages abroad. Take, for example, some of the most remarkable Swiss of today: Ferdinand Hodler, C. F. Ramuz, Blaise Cendrars, C. G. Jung, Karl Barth, Emile Jaques-Dalcroze and Arthur Honegger.

Ferdinand Hodler died in 1918, at the age of 65 years, but his influence still dominates almost all living Swiss painting. His was doubtless the most authentically native genius that Switzerland has produced in the contemporary period, the one which owes least to foreign influences. His real masters were the soldier-painters of the Renaissance and the Swiss Reformation, a Niklaus Manuel Deutsch, and an Urs Graf. It is in their exact tradition but in vastly greater proportions, and in a style that has been brutally simplified, that Hodler composed his warrior frescoes and his athletic allegories. He was a great landscapist (especially of the Alps) and a pitiless portrait painter, but it is when he portrays the Halberdiers of the Wars of Italy that he reaches his grandest form. Nothing today gives us so direct a sensation of the force of the old Confederates as the warriors of Marignano, shortlegged, thick and square, lowering their foreheads like bulls before the attack.

The prose of C. F. Ramuz has often been compared with the painting of Cézanne and of the Cubists, but in fact it is far more like the deliberate stylizing of Hodler. Ramuz is without any doubt the greatest living Swiss writer and one of the greatest French writers of our times. His novels seem to be tragedies of peasant life or epics of alpine villages, but they are not in the least the product of "naturalism" or "regionalism." His method is to reduce everything to a symbol or myth; psychological analysis is replaced by a description of forms and of motions, according to a technique which recalls that of the old silent films where atmosphere and gesture told the story without commentary. Ramuz lived in Paris for many years, alone, misunderstood, but laboring to forge himself an absolutely original style, one slow, rocky, full of pauses and new departures, like the gait of a man who climbs a steep slope. The war of 1914 brought him back to his native canton of Vaud, which he had always described in his books, but where he was read only after Paris publishers and critics gave him a reputation.

In spite of Ramuz's extreme modernism it is easy to trace his Swiss origins in his work. The taste for physical *things,* the fascinating descriptions of tools and their handling, the restraint of his novels, where the greatest passions express themselves in the smallest gestures, the solid construction of his books, all these are the qualities of a race at once Protestant and closely bound to the soil. Ramuz's influence has constantly grown both in his own country and in France. In his house by Lake Leman he receives literary pilgrims every day—but he hates to be interviewed, and he amuses himself by bombarding his visitors with questions, apparently naïve, about themselves and their way of life. This is a real peasant's trick—but it has made of Ramuz one of the best and most curiously informed men of this era.

Blaise Cendrars (his real name is Fritz Sauser-Hall) was born in Switzerland, although very few people are aware of it. He is the antithesis of Ramuz, for he is the eternal émigré, the lyrical nomad. In former days he would have enlisted in one of the regiments of the foreign service. During the first world war he fought with the Foreign Legion and lost an arm. He writes his books by means of a dictaphone, and we have seen him roll a cigarette with his left hand on the platform of a Paris bus.

He invented modern French poetry before Apollinaire and the surrealists—see his book *Easter in New York.* He introduced Negro folklore to Europe, wrote novels of adventure and epic pieces of newspaper reporting, and he has known all the world's adventurers. Today he represents the Swiss "irregulars." Irrepressible and hard-boiled, neither teacher nor moralist, but a poet, and a poet of the most extravagant action, he recalls the turbulent geniuses of the Swiss Renaissance such as Dr. Paracelsus, who wandered across Europe from inn to university, followed by his band of quarrelsome disciples, or Niklaus Manuel Deutsch, who was alternately painter, warrior, playwright and statesman. Like them and like Honegger in music, he has the gift of creative improvisation, based however on a sound technique and shrewd practical sense.

Carl Gustav Jung is too well known in America to need lengthy introduction. His work as a psychoanalyst overflows that of Freud, which it corrects and enriches. It has turned more and more towards a kind of religious quest. Jung is a doctor and a professor, but he has an intimate knowledge of the religions of Africa and the Orient, which he studied on the spot. He made himself a Negro sorcerer for some months, and his enemies call him a white sorcerer today. His great discovery has been that of "constant symbols" or "archetypes," which his immense knowledge and a kind of poetical intuition led him to recognize in the rites and mysteries of cults in every time and land, in the dreams of his patients, and in the "collective subconscious" of our epoch. Jung's varied fields of investigation and his synthetic spirit ally him to a whole line of explorers of the occult: Paracelsus, Lavater, the romantic I. V. Troxler, Bachofen, and H. F. Amiel, author of the *Journal* which is the monstrous masterpiece of introspection. In these men one fundamental aspect of Swiss culture finds expression—a passionate interest in man as a moral being and a religious animal.

The theology of Karl Barth might be characterized *grosso modo* as a reaction against this religious psychology and against the Protestant liberalism of the last two centuries in general. It opposes to them the massive affirmation—alpine, one might say—of a Christianity centered not on religious feeling and the insatiable and uncertain needs of the human heart, but upon God the "utterly different." In his own way, Barth is a great fighter, a Swiss warrior of the early days. His "commentary on the Epistle to the Romans" which he wrote for his personal use while he was the clergyman of a village near the Rhine during the war of 1914 was published by a few friends just after the war. Its success was immediate, and it produced a deep impression throughout intellectual Germany. Barth was utterly amazed by this. He felt himself, he said, to be like a man who in the darkness of a belfry staircase clutches at the bannister to guide himself and finds that he has pulled the bell-rope and brought together all the congregation!

Appointed to a professorship in Germany he became in spite of himself the head of a school of thought. Barth brought about in ten years or so a revival of the orthodoxy of the Reformers which wakened Protestant thought throughout the world. It is on the basis of a doctrine drawn from his teachings and his direct action that the German Confessional

Church (*Bekenntniskirche*) was founded. Today with its 6,000 clergyman it is the rampart of inner resistance to pagan Hitlerism. A year after the Führer came to power, Barth was called before the law-courts and deprived of his professorship. He was accused of having spoken against the régime in private homes. His only defense was to read to his judges the "Farewell of Socrates." In the spring of 1940 when the German threat to Switzerland became acute he enlisted as a volunteer in the auxiliary services, although he was fifty-four years old. Barth is considered by Catholics as well as Protestants to be the greatest living theologian. He is of the race of the Reformers, and in stature he is not unworthy of them.

In Emile Jacques-Dalcroze we find the good-humored and fantastic side of the Swiss, or more precisely of the French Swiss, character. Dalcroze is known everywhere as the creator of a new method of teaching music, the "rhythmic," in which the whole body is used, and harmony of sound is translated by that of motion. Dalcroze Institutes exist in every capital, and the one in New York is particularly flourishing. But "Monsieur Jaques," as his friends call him, is also a prolific composer, and the author of several hundred songs, some patriotic, some sentimental, some written for children, which are extremely popular in Switzerland and in France. In music and words alike he has known how to express the easy-going humor, and the deep feeling for nature of the

French-Swiss college student that he has never ceased to be. Dalcroze's songs have already become a part of the folklore of Switzerland. You hear them in schools, in student clubs, in alpine huts, on the roads, and around the fires which are lit on the first of August on the heights to commemorate the oath of the Rütli. There are few examples of an artistic career which has been so intimately blended with the life of a whole people, which has become so national, during the life of the composer.

Many people are unaware that Dalcroze is a composer, but still more fail to realize that Arthur Honegger is Swiss. He was, in fact, born in Le Havre, and has spent a large part of his life in France, but he was a Swiss soldier, and he speaks the dialect of his own canton fluently. His music itself attests a certain fundamental Helvetianism by its solid proportions and its sincerity. The biblical inspiration of his oratorios is itself a Swiss trait. Did not Ramuz once say that the Bible is the real "antiquity" of that country, much more living for its inhabitants than the Gallo-Roman past? What differentiates Honegger from other contemporary musicians is a basic equilibrium—of which he gives an impression physically—and an almost classic conception of creation in art. No one is less prone to yield to undisciplined inspiration, no one knows better how to use the limitations imposed by surrounding conditions, such as the size of the work required and the public for which it is written. His sure craftsmanship has led him to attempt the most varied kinds of production; oratorios, operas, chamber music, music for the cinema, without becoming stiff, or allowing technique to stifle emotion. His world-wide reputation is due in part to his most doubtful work, "Pacific 231," but it is in choral music that he has produced masterpieces, and particularly in the series of oratorios from "King David" to "Nicholas de Flue." This may be because in them he returns to the great communal tradition of Swiss art, that of the Festival, which merits a separate treatment.

VIII. FESTIVAL

SWITZERLAND has given the world of art no individuals of absolutely first rank, as Holland gave it Rembrandt, and Saxony, Bach. But it has created an artistic *genre* which is original and in which it excels because this genre translates the communal genius of the Confederation and illustrates the very *raison d'être* of that State. This is the Festival, or *Festspiele*.

It is sometimes thought that the jodel is the typically Swiss art form. But the jodel is typical of Switzerland only in the way in which the Negro spirituals may be said to be typical of the United States. It is not so much a Swiss specialty as a bizarrerie. It exists only in certain regions of Switzerland, and it is also to be found in many other countries—even in Thibet.

Paul Budry writes: "If Switzerland has created anything original it is the jodel. In its very design, in its wide intervals, in its rising notes and its lace-work of tones the jodel seems to reproduce the configuration of the Alps whose echoes it rouses." [1] But the same writer admits that the jodel is alpine rather than Swiss. "It expresses the pure exuberance, the

[1] P. Budry: *La Suisse qui Chante.*

exaltation which fills the soul in the ozonated air of the heights, that air which literally draws the yell from the throat. It is the thrill of giddiness itself . . . In the mountains of India our *Ruguusser*[2] are sung under the name of *ragasses.* One might perhaps trace the path of the jodel across the continents, as it moves from altitude to altitude at the height of the upper pasturages." The jodel, of which tradition tells as early as the fourth century of our era, before the Christianization of Switzerland, was probably at first a magical invocation, not an art.

"These airs with their continual high and low notes, going from the top to the bottom of the voice, with their long holds on top notes, where the voice begins as it were to wink on a trill, their descending chromatic cascades, gliding like an eagle from the heights to the depths—their pattern, which the singer varies at will by different vocal tonalities; bellowings, clarinet-like nasal sounds, violin-like scrapings, which are accompanied by the sound of a mouth organ or of a coin shaken in a bowl, are obviously intended, like all primitive chants, to daze the public, and conjure away something—silence, fear, solitude, a demon, or the terror of Man exposed in the loneliness of the Alps to the menace of the air. He sings—he sings frantically with all his might, shaking his little bells to ward off present terror. The jodel is a creation of the desert heights, where reassuring civilization has

[2] A word in the dialect of Appenzell.

not yet quite dispersed the phantoms of the *Servan,* and the *Old Man of the Mountain* who sets fire to the chalet and brings pestilence and panic to the flocks. You will find the jodel, together with the alpine horn, everywhere at timber-line." [3] It might be added that most of the jodels which are sung in foreign countries or registered for the phonograph are mild and disciplined versions of the authentic "roaring" which is improvised with endless variety by the herdsmen of Appenzell.

The Festival is, on the contrary, an historical art form, which has developed slowly in the course of a long evolution. It expresses in a high degree the soul and the common customs of the whole Swiss people. "The Festival may be defined as a work created by and for the people. This means that it must appeal to the people as a whole, and that the executants must be drawn from among the population itself. The necessary artistic elements are an important musical score, a brilliant setting, many participants, games and perhaps dances."

The stage of a Festival is built especially for the occasion, and is made of several parts or levels connected by broad stairways, in order to allow the free movement of actors and choruses. Often as many as four or five hundred, perhaps a thousand or more, persons take part. The Vaudois Festival of 1903 included 2,500 actors. These Festivals are given as a

[3] P. Budry, *Op. cit.*

rule out of doors or else in improvised tents, and huge crowds come to them. They are almost always given to celebrate a patriotic anniversary or some special event of cantonal or Federal significance, such as an Exhibition, a great shooting match, or a meeting of gymnastic or choral societies. There is almost no celebration of any importance, civic or religious, which does not give rise to a Festival composed by a poet and a musician for that special occasion.

The authors have a new problem to work out each time, for in preparing their work they must consider on the one hand the resources of the canton or city which has requested their services, and on the other the historical or allegorical significance of the particular festivity. Whether it is the memory of a battle that is to be celebrated, or the entrance of a canton into the Confederation, or some hero of the past, a certain historical accuracy is required of the playwright, for the audience will be thoroughly familiar with the subject, and will want to see the traditional events and characters on the stage. The choral groups play a part rather like that of the choruses in Greek tragedy; they comment on the action, express in lyrical form the feelings of the public, and represent in contrast to the individual heroes the collective element, the crowd, which is sometimes a spectator, sometimes (as in the case of battles or processions) a participant in the drama. The divisions of the stage, the size of the choruses, the quality of the actors, who are always amateurs, the budget allowed for decoration and costumes are so many factors which the poet and even the musician must take into account. These vary greatly from one canton to another. The authors always work in close collaboration with the local committees which are in charge of the Festival, and which are supposed to raise the money, choose the actors and give the celebration the necessary official sanction. It is obvious that these Festivals are genuinely communal creations. The work is done by groups, and it makes use of all the resources of the place where it is given. It requires an enthusiastic co-operation, and often when the subject is historical it brings about a sort of truce among the political parties.

But the composition of a Festival is not entirely arbitrary. This type of creation has its own laws, which can be traced back to its origins. The Festival was probably born from the conjunction of two distinct parts which had each followed a parallel evolution: the procession and the cantata.

It has been said that the Swiss have processions in the blood. They love their local costumes, and they like to wear the clothes and armor of their ancestors in public on great occasions. To do so is not a masquerade nor a carnival, but the plastic representation of a past which to them is still very living. They go to the Landesgemeinde, their congress, in a procession, and the meeting is carried on like a drama—or rather like one of the old mystery plays of the

Middle Ages. The procession reaches the market place and forms the "ring," a circle symbolic of the Alliance. The ceremony is opened and closed by prayer, the alternating speeches of the orators form a sort of dramatic dialogue, and the applause or protests of the crowd give a first idea of the spoken chorus. There we have the elements of the Festival.

The Fête des Vignerons, which is given every twenty-five years at Vevey, also originated in a procession, that of the workers in the vineyards going to get their official rewards. Little by little in the course of the eighteenth century, this procession was enriched by allegorical personages such as Bacchus, the goddesses Ceres and Pallas, groups of harvesters and bacchantes, representing the seasons. From 1778 on, the procession stopped at one place or another to show the public the popular dances. Later it was brought into an arena where a sort of ordered game took place. Musical interludes soon appeared, and a poet was requested to write the words of the songs and invocations. The Festival thus reached its ultimate form, which has not changed since the beginning of the nineteenth century.

Music was, of course, essential for the expression of collective emotions, and the Swiss love of choral singing, the numerous *Männerchor* (male choruses) which exist in the villages, furnish the composers with the necessary resources. "Put two Swiss together," says Paul Budry, "and the second will at once strike up an alto; put three together and the third will undertake a bass. This is Swiss polyphony, the natural music of our mystical federation. Weak when it is a question of melody alone, our song takes on its full meaning when the voices are polyphonic."

But the Festival is not only a federal art by its origins and its laws but also by its social function. In fact, it is a much-needed element in the formation of the civic consciousness of Swiss democracy. *No human society worthy of the name can do without celebrations.* That is what the totalitarians have so well understood in our day, after centuries of individualism in which the social bond had become dangerously loose because of the lack of common symbols, common emotions, and the common celebration of the great memories and enduring values of the nation. But totalitarian celebrations are almost always sad, with a military and geometrical appearance. The crowds watch them, but can only take part in them by mechanically rhythmic cheers.

The Festival, on the contrary, puts on the stage highly individual heroes, known and loved by the people whose ideal of liberty they incarnate. These heroes are not surrounded by anonymous and rigidly disciplined performers, but by choruses with whom they dialogue and communicate—that is to say, by real *communities.* Each of these Festivals is a great patriotic event in the canton. Special trains bring the spectators from the farthest parts of the country. The chief political authorities and the officers of the highest rank attend the first performance officially. The press gives free publicity, and comments at length on the civic lessons to be drawn from the work. The folklore of the region is enriched by the songs and music, which the *Männerchor* popularize throughout the country. By its effect on the people the Swiss Festival is, in fact, a direct expression of living federalism. It is impossible to stress too much its sociological importance, to insist too much on the lessons which modern democracies should draw from it if they want to escape the double peril of a dissolving individualism and of a collectivist reaction of the totalitarian type.

The influence of the Festival has done much to develop a taste for the theater in Switzerland. Not, however, for the theater of the city, which is born in closed halls and caters to a predominantly middle class public. The centers of Swiss theatrical activity lie not in the cities but at Einsiedeln, the famous monastery of central Switzerland, where they present each year a certain number of great plays, such as Calderon's "Theater of the World," which has never been given anywhere else; at Selzach, a little village in the canton of Soleure, known for its Passion Play; at Mézières, a hamlet of the canton of Vaud where a vast wooden theater which looks like a farmhouse has been built; and at the Goetheanum, at Dornach, near

Basel, the temple of the Anthroposophs, where they gave each year a remarkable performance of the second part of Goethe's "Faust." It is true that the Fête des Vignerons was held in the market place of the little city of Vevey, but it celebrated the labor of fields and vineyards, and the greater part of the participants were agricultural workers and amateurs recruited in the countryside. The theater at Mézières played a great part in the movement that developed a new type of stage scenery which was later used by the Theâtre du Vieux Colombier in Paris. The Mézières theater made use of the choral societies of the neighboring villages, aided by students and volunteers from Lausanne. It was with such local and popular elements that Honegger's masterpiece, "King David," was given for the first time.

In no country are there more amateur theatricals than in Switzerland. Every local society, every parish club, every political or philanthropic group, even the various units of the army in times of mobilization, get up plays. Naturally the artistic level varies very much, but people always put their heart into these performances, and the real fervor which goes into the preparation of "theatrical evenings," animates the whole community and gives it a new sense of its own coherence.

The small village group of amateur actors grows little by little into the Festival, and the latter becomes a great patriotic celebration. In his *Green*

Henry Gottfried Keller describes a performance of Schiller's "Wilhelm Tell" by the population of the primitive cantons. It was played not only out of doors but in "all the country," that is to say in the very places where Schiller, according to history, had placed the legendary action of the hero. Bands of peasants in costume, some on foot, others on horseback, wander through the regions around the Lake of the Four Cantons. At the given moment Tell meets the bailiff, Gessler, in the hollow road of Küssnacht. At last everyone assembles on the meadow of the Rütli for the scene of the oath. After this they light a beacon-fire, as did the first Confederates on August 1, 1291, and soon thousands of fires glow on every mountain and hill in Switzerland.

This unanimous performance, in which both nature and the people take part, this immense work of art which mingles the living past with the present, elevating the concrete reality of the whole country to the height of its eternal myth, this spectacle-in-action on an extraordinary scale is not the dream of a visionary poet. Even as we write these lines, it is actually taking place in the same spot as of old, in the holy places of the Confederation, to celebrate the Six Hundred and Fiftieth Anniversary of the Oath and the Perpetual Pact.

We cannot do better than to reproduce here the program of these festivities, just as it was published by the Swiss press. In it are gathered all the elements of the Festival as we have sketched it; an historical celebration and procession in which the people and the authorities take part, the participation of various societies and of the cantonal governments, and at the end the Oath, which is generally the high point of these evocations.

"CELEBRATION OF THE 650TH ANNIVERSARY OF THE SWISS CONFEDERATION

"At midnight of July 21st, at the Rütli, in the presence of a representative of the Federal Council and of Torchbearers coming from every canton, the federal fire will be lit by the three Landamanns of the cantons which formed the primitive Confederation. At this fire the torchbearers of every canton will light their torches to carry them to Brunnen, whence they will be taken across the lake to the chief cities of their respective cantons. The runners will hand on the fire of the Rütli so that the flame which our fathers lit 650 years ago in the heart of the original Switzerland may continue to burn in every part of the Swiss Confederation with an equal light. The torchbearers of the nearest cantons will wait at Brunnen until the signal is given for their departure. Those of the remoter cantons will leave at once, bearing their message. The Swiss Association for Physical Development has undertaken to organize this torch race.

"On the morning of August 1st, the Festivities will open with a salute of 22 cannon and the ringing of the church bells in Schwytz. In the afternoon the official guests will meet at Seewen. All the members of the Federal Council, delegations from the Federal Assembly, from the Federal Tribunal, from the Tribunal of Insurances and other Federal authorities, the Governments of the primitive cantons, and representatives of the Governments of all the other cantons, the General and other heads of the Army, the representatives of the Churches and of the youth of the Universities, as well as the troops chosen for this service of honor will all take part in the commemoration.

"From Seewen the procession will go to Schwytz and the Landamann will receive the official guests in the square before the Town Hall and will greet the people in the name of Schwytz and of Primitive Switzerland, after which, before the parade of the troops, the General will greet the country in the name of the Army. Immediately after this the new frescoes in the Archives of Schwytz will be unveiled, and a monument to the Swiss National defense, given by a group of Swiss abroad, will be presented.

"From 7:45 P.M. to 8:00 o'clock in Schwytz and throughout Switzerland the bells will ring for the general celebration. At 8 o'clock this celebration will begin in Schwytz in front of the Town Hall. The bearer of the torch with the fire from the Rütli will arrive and will light the commemorative fire of Schwytz. Exactly at the same hour, the commemorative festivities will begin in the chief cities of each canton, and the Torchbearers of the Rütli will arrive to light the fires of the 1st of August.

"At 9 o'clock the first performance of the Festival Play of César von Arx with the musical score of J. B. Hilber will begin in Schwytz. This festival play in three succeeding tableaux—the beginnings, the new developments, and the consolidation—will remind the men of 1941 of what the Confederates of 1291 have to tell them.

"The day of August 2nd will begin in Schwytz with a military religious service. At the beginning of the afternoon the population and its guests will go to the Rütli for a commemorative ceremony. The theatrical society of the 'Tell Play' of Altdorf will present the scene of the Rütli according to Schiller's 'Wilhelm Tell,' as the poet himself conceived it. After the people of Unterwald, who come first, the people of Uri and of Schwytz will come by the lake in boats, to swear an oath of fidelity and of perpetual solidarity. The words of the oath will be uttered by the whole crowd assembled at the Rütli:

> 'We swear we will be a nation of true brothers
> Never to part in danger or in death;
> We swear we will be free, as were our fathers
> And sooner die than live in slavery.'

"After this presentation of the scene of the Rütli, a single speech will follow—that of the President of the Confederation, and the celebration will end by the singing of the Swiss Hymn. As this whole celebration will be broadcast, all our fellow citizens and all the Swiss abroad will be able to participate in it, and thus to renew in themselves the oath of 1291."

IX. THE ARMY OF A DEMOCRACY

THE United States is today face to face with an urgent problem; it is that of defending democracy without losing its essence, without falling into totalitarianism by way of militarization.

Switzerland is the one country in the world which has solved the problem, and every American should be familiar with its example, not necessarily to imitate it, but to find there possibilities, suggestions, and perhaps a new confidence. Here are the facts:

First, Switzerland is the best armed democracy in the world. With a population of 4,300,000 souls, it keeps up an army of nearly 600,000 men. This means that one out of every seven inhabitants becomes a soldier on the day of general mobilization. The same proportion would give the United States an army of about 20,000,000 men.

Second, nowhere are customs and institutions more genuinely democratic than in Switzerland, and yet nowhere is the Army more popular, more essentially a part of civic life.

These two facts can be explained by the military and civic tradition of the cantons and by the federal structure which they have been able to preserve down to our own times. The example of Switzerland shows that a democracy in our days can be militarily strong only if it is openly and thoroughly democratic, even in the details of its organization and its political habits.

Shortly before the war of 1914 the Emperor William II paid an official visit to the Swiss government. While assisting at the military maneuvers, he said to one of the soldiers, "You are 500,000, and you shoot well, but if we attack you with a million men, what will you do?" "We will each fire twice," answered the soldier calmly. The Kaiser preferred to pass through Belgium.

An interesting anthology could be made of the tributes paid to the military value of the Swiss by heads of States and great captains from Louis XIV and Frederick II to Napoleon. Such a book would be all the more surprising in that the name of Switzerland is associated for us in modern times with the idea of peace. The flag which bears a red cross on a white ground has made us forget the flag with a white cross on a red ground, from which it originated. Was it not because Switzerland was always able to defend its independence by arms that it gave birth to the pacific work of the Red Cross?

From the earliest times the Swiss were free because they were strong, but also, as we shall see, they were strong only because they were free. Civil liberty and a military spirit not only have never been in contradiction in that country but rather they have created each other. What is the secret of this curious paradox?

To understand it, we must go back to one of the oldest customs of the Germanic Middle Ages. At that time the "free man," that is to say the man who enjoyed civil rights and was not the serf of a lord, was distinguished by one fact—he had the right to carry arms—just as the nobles were later distinguished by the wearing of a sword. From the moment that the Swiss communes first freed themselves from the yoke of the Barons and came to depend only on the Imperial Crown the proportion of free men became large. The Swiss valued their weapons as tokens of their liberty. Since then and throughout the centuries their army has always been a gathering of free citizens, each of whom possesses his own arms and proudly cares for his rifle, his ammunition, and his military equipment. In Switzerland one often sees in the poorer neighborhoods uniforms hanging out on the balcony to be "aired," or a peasant sitting on the threshold of his farmhouse polishing and greasing his gun after the Sunday sharp-shooting. You will see this nowhere else in the world, for Switzerland is the only country where this medieval custom has lasted without interruption down to our own day.

The possession by each citizen of his own individual weapon shows in the most concrete possible way that the State trusts its citizens absolutely and that they have reached a degree of civic maturity unrivaled elsewhere. Imagine what would happen in certain modern States torn by social or political struggle if the demobilized soldiers were allowed to take home their arms and their ammunition! In France after the Armistice of 1940 the soldiers were offered 1,000 francs in exchange for their rifles for fear of revolutionary troubles. Hitler had his own shock troops disarmed after the purge of June 30, 1934, leaving them only a decorative dagger. Even in America the theft of arms from one of the arsenals of the militia was a source of grave anxiety.

But the possession of individual weapons is not only a sign of freedom and responsibility; it also has a technical importance which the present war has shown to be considerable. It is the only method which permits of an ultra-rapid and decentralized mobilization. Thus medieval custom has become the most modern method of defense, the one best fitted to protect a country against a Blitzkrieg.

In France as in Germany when people speak of the Army the word brings a vision of a world wholly alien to civilian life. The Swiss do not say "the Army" but rather "the military," as though they were speaking of one part of their normal lives, the military one. To hear the French, at least before this war, the Army and the time spent in it were fit subjects for jokes and for grumbling. It was against the life of barracks and against the adjutant that the French citizen, even if he was conservative and anti-pacifist, exercised his individualistic spirit, his refusal to be overawed by collective discipline. In Germany, on the contrary, the Army was something solemn and sacred, a sort of weighty religion which could endure no hint of skepticism.

For the Swiss the Army is simply "service" and that is how they refer to the time spent in the school of recruits and in the "rehearsal periods," the annual schools of training and maneuvers lasting four weeks which are required of all mobilizable men. Simply "the service." The expression itself is very enlightening as to the conception which the citizens of this democracy have of their military duties. They do not take them tragically nor do they make fun of them. They are simply a part of their lives just as are their professions or their families.

When Swiss men meet, whether it is in a café, a train, or some foreign city where accident has brought them together, you may be sure that as an opening and in order to make better acquaintance they will at once ask each other about their "service." "The last stage I made in the Army was in the plain of Seeland—you know—the big maneuvers of the second division in 1934 when the Colonel was taken prisoner." "Oh," says the other, "I was there, too! I belong to the 204th battalion—Major Schmidt. You know him? What is your battalion?" And dates are compared and the good old classical jokes, as well known as the words of command, are trotted out. One always ends by finding common acquaintances in the service. Confidence is established and the second round of drinks ordered.

But the Army is a bond not only between individuals, but also between classes. Switzerland has no exclusive schools for officers such as the cadet schools in Germany, St. Cyr in France or West Point in America. All young men of twenty who are fit for service must attend the same school of recruits even though they are destined some day to rise to the highest rank. There, during four months of intensive technical and moral training, they live through a social experience which will leave its mark on them for the rest of their lives. The peasant has for roommate or neighbor in the ranks the spectacled student; the workman has the son of his boss. During four months of ordeals and fatigues there is time to watch each other, to discover the real strength and weakness of one's neighbors and to make a few lasting friendships. A complete, though sometimes rather cross-grained, equality exists in the barracks, and often manifests itself as at school in practical jokes played on the young man of good family or on the nephew of the Colonel in command. This education, rough enough, and accompanied by a physical training methodically carried on, sends these men back to civilian life quite visibly transformed; straightened, bronzed, hardened, yet made supple, endowed also with an experience of men which the over-peaceful life of the city or village would not have given them in ten years.

This system of a school of recruits with its periods of brief but intensive training seems to have notable advantages over that practiced elsewhere, of one to three years' service in barracks or camps. Because the time is short the recruits are not allowed to lose a minute. Whereas the two years of military instruction are too often a school of demoralization and of lost time for young Frenchmen, these four months of the school of recruits are a powerful tonic for Swiss youths and the model of a swift and well-ordered life in which one's forces are used to the utmost all the time. On the other hand the shortness of the period allows each recruit to find his place in civilian life waiting for him when he goes back, which would not be the case after one or two years. Thus one of the major reasons for the unpopularity of army life in other countries disappears.

As to the technical insufficiency which must result from so brief a period of service, it is to a large extent compensated for by the yearly period of rehearsal. Some experts, and even some Swiss politicians, have for years demanded a prolongation of the school of recruits, but until now popular opinion has opposed this. The Swiss like the military life but they are not militaristic. Instinctively they fear everything that might make of the Army too technical a body and one too remote from the normal life of the nation.

The Swiss Army is organized so as to "decivilize" the citizen as little as possible, but on the other hand civilian life brings him frequent and living contacts with military affairs. There are in every canton "friendly circles" of officers and non-commissioned officers; in every village shooting clubs exist. Many of these associations, and particularly those of non-commissioned officers, have acquired a certain political influence in the country. But it must be emphasized that this influence is not "militaristic." Such groups are rather like the public discussion clubs which exist in other democracies. To have been in the Army, to have common memories of it, is the pretext for getting together among comrades to discuss the affairs of the country in an atmosphere saner and more virile than that of political parties. Thus these "friendly societies," far from being Fascist centers as might be feared, have up to now had a stabilizing and moderating influence on public life.

As for the body of officers, it is not at all a caste, as it has tended to become in other countries. The very method of recruiting prohibits that. The Swiss officer is in most cases a civilian like the rest except that this civilian must be able to become a leader from one day to the next and to command his men in the maneuvers. This happens every year at the time of the rehearsal period.

In between times, he must give several hours a week from his professional occupations to the many duties of his military rank. A Captain, for instance, still looks after his company in civilian life. He always knows where his men live. A scrupulously observed custom requires them to send him their good wishes at the New Year and these he always answers. Many of them turn to him for advice or for help in finding work. All consider him as the head of a big family of 200 men.

The daily press, the magazines, the illustrated papers give a great deal of space to military affairs, a fact which always strikes foreigners. Reporters accompany the troops at each rehearsal period and send detailed accounts of the maneuvers from day to day to their papers. The nomination of officers is given space on the first page, and Swiss death notices always tell the details of a man's military career. Thus, we may discover that such and such a judge, doctor, university professor, or big business man was also a Colonel, which means that he had voluntarily dedicated several years of his life to the Army.

To be a Colonel in Switzerland is to occupy a position which has no equivalent in other countries, one social as well as military, and which might be said to be a civic function. A man who has reached the rank of Colonel will not always have a triple chin and a bay window figure, as caricatures imply, but he probably enjoys a popularity greater than that of a Congressman and has also in all probability a sound financial standing. He has certainly given proof of political wisdom and of considerable activity. His professional influence will undoubtedly be greater than that of his colleagues.

A particular case will illustrate the above. It is that of the General. In Switzerland the officer commanding a brigade, a division, or an Army corps, is only a Colonel, for there is a certain republican mistrust of too sonorous names. Only when the mobilization is decreed does the Parliament choose one of the Colonels commanding an Army corps to be General-in-Chief. This one General at once becomes the symbol of the Army, the first citizen and the most important person in the country. The twenty-two cantonal governments in turn invite him to lunch, crowds acclaim him wherever he goes, his photograph is seen in all shops and public places. He is visible everywhere in busts, medals, postcards, on embroidered sofa cushions, and on packages of chocolate. He talks over the radio, he writes prefaces for patriotic books, he opens fairs, goes to football matches, skiing competitions, and first nights at the theaters. One might almost imagine that the Swiss democracy is indulging in the cult of a Führer! But not at all. Everyone knows that there is no danger. The fact that the Parliament elected this leader is a guarantee of his fidelity to the

Constitution. That he will automatically give up his powers as soon as his mission is over (that is to say, at the demobilization) is proof that the fundamental tradition of European democracy still lives: this is to name a leader when certain definite needs arise but to name him freely and only for a strictly limited time. The Swiss General is not a Hitler but a Cincinnatus. Is not the fact that the Swiss democracy can afford to give such power to one man in times of crisis and can do so without risk to its national institutions the best possible sign of a thoroughly wholesome civic life?

The possession of arms by the individual is linked with the tradition of local defense and the latter is in turn the product of the conformation of Swiss territory. Each canton in the course of its history has had its own battles, fought alone, to win its independence. Each, therefore, has learned to develop its own particular system of defense according to its topography and resources. Flat countries require large armies, rapid movements, and a dynamic strategy. A country all in small compartments, like Switzerland, does not lend itself to this sort of warfare. Small bodies of men raised on the spot suffice to defend the deep valleys and to bar the passage of narrow gorges and high defiles. It is a question of a firm morale and skillful tactics. If the enemy is too powerful, reinforcements are asked of the neighbors with whom all has long been prearranged. Thus we find at the basis of the military organization the same factors which determine the political structure of the country; that is, local autonomy and mutual aid. No more of great strategy than of great political policy but a tenacious and skillful use of every least advantage which the terrain and the arms at hand allow.

Most of the cantons correspond *grosso modo* to the natural divisions of the soil. The *cantonal* organization of the Army down to the scale of the regiment thus corresponds practically with the military needs, although it originated in far-off historic causes. It is the government of the cantons which recruits the men and names the officers up to the rank of Captain. Thus in a Swiss regiment you will find as a rule men coming from the same part of the country, speaking the same dialect and for the most part knowing each other. As to the larger units, brigades and divisions, they group regiments from neighboring cantons in such a way that each corresponds to what might be called in military terms "territorial compartments." The officers of higher rank are appointed by the Federal Council. They must know at least two languages, French and German, so that they may command the troops of the various cantons which are grouped under their orders.

In this way, the scheme of military organization is like the political one, and both correspond approximately to the natural divisions of Switzerland. Switzerland has never created a centralized Army according to a theoretical plan. On the contrary, all is founded on local units which have been co-ordinated ever more closely during the centuries. Today unity of command is complete, but the cantonal divisions are used and respected. Each regiment keeps its particular character and customs. The Bernese are strict in discipline, the Neuchâtellois are grumblers, but they know how to extricate themselves from every trouble, the Genevese march more rapidly than the Vaudois, but the latter believe that they can march longer, etc. Each has its songs, its fanfares, its jokes, and its own appearance.

As to the battle order of the Swiss Army, it also has certain peculiarities which are very interesting today. The Army is composed of nine regular divisions, organized into four Army corps. These divisions form the mass which can be maneuvered, the mobile part of the Army. The rest of the forces—almost a half—consists first of garrisons which are established in the forts that defend the principal passages of the Alps, those of the Gothard, of St. Maurice en Valais, of the Sargans; second, of the mountain brigades, specialists in skiing and alpinism in the Valais and the Grisons; and lastly of a certain number of independent brigades, the defenders of the frontiers, which are the most typically Swiss units of the Army because of their recruiting and function.

These frontier guards are recruited locally, that is

to say, the men who compose them are chosen from the cities, villages and farms nearest to the positions which have been prepared on the frontier. They know these positions well for they have themselves arranged them, hollowed them out, cemented them, and fortified them with their own hands. They know how to reach them in one to three hours of march from their own homes. At the first alarm these troops are warned directly by radio, telephone, or telegram, or by the ringing of the tocsin. All that they have to do is to put on their uniforms, take up their rifles, and go to their posts of combat by the very paths which they are in the habit of using. They will find machine guns or anti-tank cannon ready on the spot. Stores of ammunition and food have been hidden in the rocks where they are protected from bombardment. All is ready. In 1939, the placing of these covering troops which preceded the general mobilization by five days was carried out in a few hours upon the whole circumference of the Swiss frontiers.

All this had been prepared over a period of ten years by the Swiss General Staff, which had foreseen exactly what a Blitzkrieg would be. This is the only effective answer to the new form of attack, which is upset by such an almost instantaneous mobilization. Why is it, then, that it has been used only in Switzerland and that so many other countries, such as Poland and Jugoslavia, have allowed themselves to be surprised and disorganized in the first hours of the attack? The answer is obvious. Switzerland was able to prepare its defense against the Blitzkrieg because it was the only country where the men were already equipped and armed in peacetime. Thus once again it is to its own democratic tradition that the Confederation owes the fact that it is able to meet modern methods of warfare.

The moral advantage of this organization is almost as important as its technical ones. Every Swiss soldier has before his eyes his reasons for living and for dying. These frontier guards take up their fighting positions within a few miles of their own homes. They know exactly what they are defending; they see it at the foot of that mountain on which they have dug their fortifications, in that valley which they can contemplate during the long watches of the night. There is no need to make speeches to them, to explain the reasons of the effort required of them. Two gestures are enough, the one to point out the frontier before them, the other to show behind them their own village, their fields or their workshops, and the roads which lead to their daily labor. One of the authors of this book was mobilized in 1939 in a frontier post of the Jura. Every morning when the weather was fine, he could take his field glass and, looking through the loophole of the fort, see a certain orchard by the lake 3,000 feet below, where he could sometimes catch a glimpse of a light summer dress or fancy that he recognized his children—such things count in the warfare of today. This is a revolutionary war and therefore as much moral as physical. Probably in the long run it will be the strongest feelings and the deepest convictions which will win. The secret of the Swiss Army is that it has preserved and encouraged the moral factor by a skillful adaptation of tactics to the physical and the human nature of the country.

It should be added that the local use of frontier guards and in a lesser degree of the regular troops is valuable also against sabotage and spying. A stranger is soon detected where the soldiers know the inhabitants and the dialect of the country. In the spring of 1940, when there was much talk of the danger of German parachutists, a Swiss observer was obliged to jump out of his plane as a result of an accident to the engine. He came down with his parachute into an apple tree in the canton of Thurgovia, an agricultural region near the German frontier. While he was trying to extricate himself from his parachute straps the peasants of the neighborhood, armed with pitchforks and scythes, surrounded the tree. The officer was wearing a Swiss uniform but there had been stories in the newspapers of the campaign in Holland and the peasants were mistrustful. "Certainly I come from this canton!"

"Can you prove it?" The poor fellow had to pass a complete examination in the oaths of the Thurgovian dialect, a tongue in which no one could swear correctly unless he had learned to do so with his mother's milk. Only then was he allowed to come down from his tree.

The question remains as to whether a small army can ever successfully defend a country against an adversary twenty, not to say fifty, times as well equipped. The examples of Norway, of Holland, of Jugoslavia, and of Greece seem to give a crushingly unanimous answer to this question. Yet these examples have not at all demoralized the Swiss soldiers. The lightning victories of the Axis have only made them repeat: "It would not happen that way with us!" They have certain reasons for thinking this which we will examine.

The first act of the Blitzkrieg is to impede or break up the mobilization of the invaded country. This cannot be done in Switzerland. Of course, the enemy air force could easily disorganize the railway communications which are almost entirely electrified and therefore depend on a few central power plants that are highly vulnerable. Switzerland possesses four hundred pursuit planes which have proved their efficiency. In the spring of 1940, they brought down ten or more big German bombers which thought to travel peacefully over Swiss territory. Nonetheless, the Axis could use forces ten or twenty times superior, and would gain the mastery of the air in a few days, possibly in a few hours, as it has done elsewhere. But this would not be decisive. In the first place, the Swiss Army has been permanently mobilized ever since 1939. In the next place, the distances are so small that troops could be moved without using the railroads. Finally, the nature of the terrain is not favorable to the effective use of airplanes in battle.

The second phase of the Blitzkrieg is the piercing and the exploitation in depth of the territory behind the lines. Would this be possible in Switzerland? To describe or foresee the condition of a war in that country, we must always come back to those two fundamental facts, the breaking up of the territory into compartments and the decentralized structure of the Army. Now recent events seem to indicate that these elements, which might have been considered weaknesses in the past, are the only conditions which lend themselves to an effective resistance to mobilized attack. What, in fact, have been the lessons of the present war? First, we have seen the total failure of the line system of defense. Neither the Mannerheim Line in Finland nor the Maginot Line in France nor the Metaxas Line in Thrace was able to resist for more than a few days, sometimes a few hours, the penetration, prepared by an intense Stuka bombardment, of the armored divisions.

Once the line was pierced, nothing was left in the hinterland but a great empty space, a few policemen, and an amorphous mass of fugitives encumbering the roads. Nothing was left to prevent the destruction of the lines of communication, the seizure of cities and arsenals by a few tanks. This system of linear defense corresponds to the structure of highly centralized nations such as France, in particular, which has a Capital and customs barriers, but nothing between these two, no living regional centers at all.

In Switzerland, on the contrary, there are as many centers of resistance as there are cantons or villages, as many bases of defense solidly organized as there are defiles and mountains. Since the month of May, 1940, it may be said that every Swiss village, even in the heart of the country, has been transformed into a sort of autonomous fort or bastion. Its entrances and exits are closed by enormous barricades several yards deep made of tree trunks and blocks of stone, and the walls of certain houses have been re-enforced so as to transform them into miniature fortresses. You open the door of some barn and find yourself face to face with an anti-tank cannon protected by a little cement wall. A rapid advance of motorized divisions could only be made by avoiding the villages and passing through forest roads or over the meadows. But the roads are carefully mined in every direction throughout the country. The forests, particularly those along the Rhine, are the best obstacle there is to the advance of tanks and the best protection against airplane bombardment. Where there are no forests, other natural obstacles exist every four or five miles: deep and rapid streams, valleys and gorges protected by cannon hidden in the rocky walls. In each "compartment" of the territory the enemy would have to stop and develop a formal attack. There would be no question of pushing rapidly along, as in the plains of Flanders or Poland. Even dive-bombing would be almost impossible in many cases because the valleys are so narrow.

"Our terrain is our best ally," General Guisan proclaimed in one of his bulletins to the Army shortly after the defeat of France. It is the great merit of Switzerland to have been able, thanks to its Federal structure, to make the utmost use of this natural ally. The great wisdom of the Swiss General Staff is to have foreseen as early as 1930 that the next war would not be one of "fronts," but would be fought everywhere at once, and that a defense must be prepared in depth, relying on nests of local resistance scattered over the territory and carefully equipped long beforehand with men and weapons. The Swiss thus returned to their old traditional way of making war.

It is very striking to find that from the beginnings of the Confederacy these scattered defense tactics were the secret of the Swiss victories over invading forces twenty times as numerous as their own. An interesting example is the battle of Morgarten, which took place in 1315.

In order to crush the cantons the Habsburgs had gathered together an army of 12,000 knights from all the neighboring countries—for the feudal lords could not tolerate in the midst of the Empire a little group of free men who claimed to be sovereign. The Swiss carefully examined the spot where they could fight with some hope of success. They built towers and mighty walls of stone across the passages which led to their territory, leaving only one road open. It was there that the Austrian column of mounted and heavily armed knights at last entered, after trying the other passes and finding them closed. The Swiss were but six hundred. Hidden behind the crests of the hills of Morgarten, above the little lake of Aegeri, they waited the passage of the knights. When these filed between the steep slopes and the shore, the mountaineers suddenly leaped out and rolled down great stones which blocked the way. The whole column was paralyzed. The rear guard was simultaneously attacked and all at once the main body of the Swiss rushed down the mountain, yelling fiercely. They had put nails in their shoes to keep from slipping on the dry grass and had fitted curved steel hooks on the ends of their long pikes. Standing solidly fixed in the soil, they were able with these hooks to harpoon and unhorse the knights, and they made a mighty carnage among them. The battle was over in a half hour if the chroniclers of the time are to be credited. It was an almost exact prefiguration of the battles in the course of which six centuries later the Finns exterminated whole brigades of Russian tanks. The Finnish tactics were also to attack the first and last tanks, and while the line was thus immobilized to fall on their flank and destroy them with anything at hand—sticks thrust into the caterpillar tread, bottles full of gasoline used as grenades. With the Swiss as with the Finns the absolute determination to defend themselves to the death coupled with a favorable terrain and an inventive spirit compensated to some extent for the great disproportion in numbers and equipment.

It is this resolution to defend themselves that must again be underlined in the case of the Swiss today. The two first years of German victory have only reinforced it. The contacts between the men and the soil, between the Army and the people, between the present and historical tradition have grown closer during this long mobilization. Never have the Swiss been more conscious of the value of their living diversity, of the reality of their union.

In May and June, 1940, during the French rout, it seemed that the sudden rupture of equilibrium of the powers would necessarily deliver Switzerland to the Axis. But Switzerland, though entirely surrounded, did not weaken. There was a wave of defeatism in the press, but the Army held firm and the population hailed with enthusiasm a proclamation signed by the Federal Council and by the General ordering all armed citizens to "act against parachutists and saboteurs with ruthless energy." Now at that time the "armed citizens" were the whole male population of the country, young and old, and many women as well. A body of "local guards" had just been created in which were included old men and boys who had not been mobilized. They were ordered to fight fire, to protect railway stations, and to attack parachutists or fifth columnists wherever they might appear. The women were volunteers organized in groups called "Lottas" which were to insure the passive anti-aircraft defense. They were given blue uniforms, a helmet, and a pair of boots, of which they showed themselves very proud.

Certainly Switzerland was spared at that time only because her neighbors of the north, east, and south understood that she would be "a hard nut to crack" and that the operation would not pay.

Four-fifths of the traffic between Germany and Italy now goes over the Gothard or the Simplon. These tunnels are mined. The explosion of two or three of the hundreds of loads of dynamite which have been prepared there would put them out of commission for years. Many men have sworn solemnly to blow them up even at the cost of their lives on the first sign of invasion. The Axis knows this.

The Axis knows, too, what the Swiss plan of defense is. To a gathering of all the higher officers in charge of the defense which was held in July, 1940, on the meadow of the Rütli, General Guisan explained this plan. The Gothard range was declared to be the national retreat, the central bastion of defense. The various units of the Army were to be ready, some to slow down the penetration of the frontiers, others, more numerous, to fall back into the valleys radiating from the Gothard. Half the territory would be sacrificed, but they would be inexpugnable and could hold out not in hope of a final victory but to save the honor of the country, the ideal of liberty and of federalism, and in order to be faithful to the mission and duty of Switzerland.

This famous "report from the Rütli" electrified the Army and the population. Nothing else was talked of anywhere. Some extracts from a speech made by Colonel Fry on April 20, 1941, before a large civilian audience at Berne, will give an idea of the state of mind of the Swiss today.

"The real Confederate is he who never asks with regard to the defense of the land, whether it pays. The true Confederate is hard and obstinate. To those who ask him, 'Why these sacrifices if they are not to benefit us in the end?' he answers, 'You miscalculate. Neither famine nor war nor deportation will be avoided if we yield without fighting. Liberty is only possible if all are free. Individual liberty cannot survive in a State which fails to defend its independence. But beyond all calculation of profit and loss there are moral values. There is the spirit. There is the federal idea which we must hand on as heritage to our descendants. That is why we will trust in God and not in a man who pretends to be adored as a God.' "

There is in this simple and unanimous resolve, in the very conception of the "plan of the Gothard" something grand and unique, something almost unhoped-for in the world of today. Imagination leads us to dream of the possible working of such a plan. We fancy an epic story of the divisions massed at the head waters of the rivers, behind narrow defiles where tanks cannot pass, dominating the land from the heights of this roof of Europe, living in tunnels and caves cut in the flanks of the Alps and invulnerable to bombardment under thousands of yards of granite and ice, impregnable, and watching day and night. The flocks of the Valais and the Grisons would be driven into the high valleys of the Gothard, to feed them. Accumulations of food and ammunition, enough for at least a year, are stored in the rocks and a powerful radio post speaks every morning to the peoples of enslaved Europe: "This is Radio-Gothard. Here we still hold out." Who knows what hidden energies the idea of this last fortress in the clouds and the voice of its cannon might waken in Europe? The world of today is looking desperately for something substantial on which to found a hope. Impregnable in the midst of chaos, the Gothard might well become our modern myth, for it is both a symbol and a reality as solid as its own granite.

X. NEUTRALITY AND AN INTERNATIONAL ROLE

THE Swiss long took their neutrality as a matter of course, or rather considered it as a sort of divine-right privilege. They have been forced by recent events to consider anew the duties and obligations, often very heavy, which are the counterpart of this privilege.

As a matter of fact neutrality is in itself unnatural, for the normal instinct of man is to take sides. It must, therefore, be justified by enduring reasons, and not by mere opportunism.

Certain so-called realists declare that Switzerland is neutral only from self-interest and because of material and utilitarian necessities; because it is so small a country; because its geographical location would expose it to so many dangers in case of war; because its racial diversity would bring about the dislocation of the Confederation if it should take part in any conflict between its neighbors. To this it can be answered that Denmark, Holland, and Greece, which are even smaller than Switzerland, were not neutral, at all events in theory. Today Switzerland is encircled by the Axis, so that the traditional arguments about a strategical or racial equilibrium between two groups of powers are no longer valid. Switzerland's purely material interest would lead it to accept the "new order" in Europe. Why does it resist so far as it can?

There can be but one answer. It is because of its European mission and the treaties which have consecrated this mission in the course of the centuries. Imposed by the defeat of Marignano, formulated by the Treaties of Westphalia in 1648, Swiss neutrality was generally accepted by European opinion in the eighteenth century. Bonaparte, after violating it himself, undertook to "protect" it by the Act of Mediation of 1803. We know well today what that word "protect" means when it is used by a despot. Yet it was, after all, an homage rendered to a fact which had become traditional. From 1815 on Swiss neutrality was an essential portion of the European equilibrium and the pivot of the entire policy of the Confederation.

However, when the League of Nations was organized on the principle of collective security, a conflict arose between the tradition of permanent neutrality and the new obligation to share in the military sanctions decreed by the League against an aggressor State. After long negotiations Switzerland at last obtained by the Declaration of London (February, 1920) the right to enter the League without participating in any military sanctions against any State or allowing the passage of foreign troops over its territory. It was only on this condition that the Swiss people approved by a federal referendum of March 16, 1920, the entry of the Confederation into the League.

That Swiss neutrality is a *unique* case in Europe and even in the world is implicitly admitted by these exceptional measures, which express the facts of a peculiar geographical situation and an historic mission that constitute the policy of this paradoxical State.

But neutrality is a function of the Swiss State and it cannot be interpreted as an individual obligation, to be imposed on each citizen.

A Swiss writer, Albert Bonnard, has said: "Swiss neutrality is a conception which applies to the State, not to the individual." Another author of authority, Philippe Godet, wrote: "There is no such thing for honest men as moral neutrality. Moral neutrality is only possible to those who have no morality. Our human duty can never be to say to our conscience when it grows indignant: 'Be still, I will not listen; you will compromise me.' A people which is reduced to such servility would pay too dear for the happiness of neutrality."

It must be admitted, however, that permanent neutrality, while it is without doubt a material privilege, brings with it certain moral dangers. It has bred in the Swiss an age-long habit of considering the struggles of their neighbors with a sort of self-righteousness which is sometimes very irritating. It has developed a politically pharisaical attitude of which the Swiss Press has given far too many examples in the last twenty-five years. It is easy to believe oneself impartial and to give advice when one is safely sheltered from blows! This moralizing attitude can only be overcome by a keen sense of the obligations which the privileges impose. "Noblesse oblige" they said in the days of the old régime, and Switzerland should often repeat to itself "neutrality obliges." This is what Carl Spitteler expressed so admirably in a speech that he made in Zurich in 1914, which has become famous. Spitteler had just won the Nobel prize. He did not hesitate to speak out, although he knew that it must lose him his wide German public:

"By our modesty we pay to wounded Europe the tribute which it is right to pay to suffering: respect. By our modesty we seek to be forgiven! Forgiven for what? . . . Those who have never been at a sick bed will not understand me. A man of heart feels the need of forgiveness for enjoying his health while others suffer. Let us above all avoid a patronizing tone—the appearance of preaching. . . .

"A special favor allows us to assist as witnesses at the fearful tragedy which is going on in Europe. In the foreground is mourning, in the background, murder. Wherever you listen, to the left or the right, you will hear pain sobbing, and the sound is the same in all languages. Well, in considering the incommensurable sum of suffering of all these peoples our duty is to let our hearts be filled with silent contemplation, and above all, to bare our heads!

"Then we will be taking the really neutral stand, the Swiss stand."

Above all Swiss neutrality must be positive. It must not be a timid and self-satisfied way of taking shelter, but, on the contrary, an opportunity for creating what the nations at war cannot create. In what way has Swiss neutrality been, according to the formula proposed by the Federal Council, "an active neutrality"?

It may be answered that the country as it exists today is, as it were, a first creation of neutrality—a "Europe reconciled with itself," as we have said. It offers a model of what the continent will perhaps be able to achieve only in centuries to come. Moreover it preserves for us certain of the fundamental values of neighboring civilizations, even when these civilizations have lost or have come for a time to despise their own proper genius. This applies particularly to German Switzerland. Even in the period after the Thirty Years' War travelers who came to it after visiting devastated Germany exclaimed that here was the refuge of the true Germanic life. The same thing can be said of it today. The deep hostility of the German Swiss to Nazism does not prevent them from feeling profoundly German in spirit and in culture—much more German than the Nazis, in particular. All that was likable in German culture, all the spicy good-humor of popular life in Swabia or on the Rhine, can be found today only in Zurich, in Basel, in Berne, or in the country about these cities. As a French Swiss author recently said, "German Switzerland, close at hand, gives us in the midst of war a providential opportunity of loving German culture in its living and human aspects. Yes—to love that civilization with perfect neutrality, with no political afterthought. It is our federal privilege to be able to enjoy in a narrow space the manifold wealth of a torn and shattered Europe."

As for French Switzerland it is an island of French Protestant culture, unique in the world. There are today four publishing houses which have established themselves in ten different cities of French Switzerland for the purpose of bringing out the works of French writers which can no longer appear in their own country.

The second creative aspect of Swiss neutrality is symbolized by the Red Cross. Switzerland is neutral, as we have shown, because it has a *super-national* mission to accomplish. Neutrality has enabled it to federate various races within its borders, in spite of their conflicts elsewhere. Its neutrality has also obliged it to become the permanent guardian of international organizations, and the protector of all future federations or attempts at federation.

About ninety international institutions have chosen one or another of the Swiss cities as their home. Such organizations as the Universal Postal Union, the Latin Monetary Union and the International Office of Industrial and Intellectual Property, settled in Switzerland before the war of 1914. After the peace of 1919 came the League of Nations, the International Labor Bureau, the Bank for International Settlements, the Oecumenical Council of Christian Churches. These few examples indicate the varied character of the organizations, European or world-wide, economic, religious, political, philanthropic, cultural or racial, which have benefited by Swiss neutrality. The papacy alone is lacking in the list of international institutions—but it is not entirely absent. Since the Vatican could not be transferred to Switzerland, the Swiss as early as the Middle Ages went to Rome! The Papal Guard is an ancient and picturesque but symbolic illustration of the international role of the Confederation. Raphael himself designed the dress and the helmet of these guards, and they are still recruited in the Catholic cantons and commanded by a Swiss Colonel.

Of all international institutions, however, the International Red Cross is the most characteristic. Not only is its headquarters in Geneva but it was the creation of a Swiss mind, and it is a direct expression of the efforts towards peace to which a neutral country may devote the talents which others dedicate to war.

It was on the battlefield of Solferino on June 29, 1859, that the first vision of the Red Cross was born in the imagination of Henry Dunant. Dunant was a young businessman of Geneva, with a generous heart and a somewhat chimerical spirit. He was not present at Solferino as a soldier, not even as a newspaperman, but as a "mere tourist," as he said. As a matter of fact he was trying to meet Napoleon III in order to give him a memoir as to the Young Men's Christian Associations, in which he took an interest. He was an immediate witness of the battle, in which 300,000 Frenchmen and Austrians took part, and which was one of the bloodiest conflicts of modern times. Thousands of dead, and tens of thousands of wounded, a day of fiery heat, no organized help for the injured, who were piled hit-or-miss into the churches of the neighboring villages. Thirst tortured them. Flies infected their wounds. The dressings were unpacked in the dust, and put on dirty straw. There was an extreme dearth of surgeons to operate and of orderlies to dress the wounds, which soon became gangrenous. Dunant made super-human efforts to help these poor wretches. He kept, however, a horrible and unforgettable impression of the fearful state to which the lack of care brought the wounded, above all those who fell into enemy hands.

Haunted by these impressions he wrote a little

book, modestly entitled *Recollections of Solferino.* The brochure ended with an impassioned appeal "to men of all countries and races who can be moved by the sufferings of their fellowmen." He proposed that a Society should be created to help wounded soldiers, one which would be recognized by all States and protected by international conventions, so that it would be able to intervene on all battlefields in any war, to help the combatants of every nationality. With the help of Genevans, among them General Defour, victor in the war of the Sonderbund, he undertook a long and difficult campaign whose object was to win the recognition of the heads of the various States for his little "International Committee for help to wounded soldiers."

"International in its action, but founded by five men of Geneva," it has been said. It was unprecedented daring for that era, but a daring which sprang from the deepest soul, and from the whole humanitarian tradition of Switzerland. In 1863 a Congress which met in Geneva ratified a charter that foresaw the formation of National Societies and of an International Committee which was to be the connecting link. They adopted as their distinguishing badge the white arm-band with a red cross on it. These were the colors and the devise of the Swiss flag, inverted. The Geneva Convention of 1864 gave its ultimate form to the Charter of the Red Cross, and made its prescriptions obligatory upon all the States which should participate.

The International Committee of the Red Cross has its headquarters in Geneva, and its personnel is recruited solely among Swiss citizens. Its twenty-five members are renewed by co-option.[1] As they are not paid they are necessarily chosen among people of a certain fortune in Geneva, or among those whom diplomatic or professional experience indicates as particularly fitted for their part. Here, then, is an institution which is entirely local in its origins and its personnel, but which, thanks to the permanent neutrality of Switzerland, is entrusted with an eminently international mission. We repeat: it is because all its members are Swiss, and so neutral by definition, that the Committee can act simultaneously on all belligerent governments. It offers them the best guarantee of independence and disinterestedness, and can inspire confidence even in the worst excitement of the struggle. In the present war the Committee of the Red Cross is the only remaining international organization which is actually functioning effectively. It is a noteworthy fact that it has won the respect of Hitler himself. He is very little inclined, as we know, to respect the institutions of Geneva, but he has been impressed by the efficiency and value of the Red Cross.

One of the principal duties of the Committee in

[1] The existing members of the board select the new members.

wartime is to create a central agency for collecting information in regard to prisoners and to arrange for communication between them and their families. During the war of 1914-1918 and in the first years of this war there have been several million prisoners in the two camps. This gives an idea of the scope of the work of the Red Cross.

That the Central Agency for Prisoners of War was ready to function in the first days of this war was due to the benevolent personal initiative of a few members of the International Red Cross Committee. Some months before war broke out they had prepared the text of a letter to be sent to each government offering the services of an organization which was foreseen in its minutest details. On September 2, as soon as hostilities were declared, the letter was sent. On September 14, as soon as the answers were received, the Agency was opened and went to work. The whole world ought to know how it functions.

We visited its offices in August, 1940. Its headquarters, which have been set up in one of Geneva's public buildings, impress one first by the extreme simplicity of their arrangements and furnishings. A large central hall surrounded by a circular gallery is occupied by a dozen rows of tables, made of boards set up on trestles. At each row some thirty persons are working. In the two wings, separated from the hall itself by thin partitions about three yards high, are a series of smaller offices. The Directors have their workrooms in another part of the building. They are the President of the Committee, Max Huber, former President of the Hague Court of Justice; his right-hand man, the writer, Jacques Chenevière, and many professors, doctors, officers of the Swiss Army, and diplomats—such as Carl Burckhardt, former High Commissioner of the League of Nations at Danzig, and well-known writer.

To return to the central hall: on its walls various signs remind the personnel of the Secretariat and their "volunteer helpers" to keep an absolute silence in regard to all letters or information which pass through their hands. The reason is clear. Here and here alone the number of prisoners, of dead and of wounded on both sides is known exactly. The revelation of these figures to one or other of the belligerents would immediately destroy the trust which both sides put in the agency.

The "voluntary collaborators" are here, and there are more than three thousand of them, whereas there are only about three hundred paid employees. It is thanks to the generous devotion of these three thousand persons and of the Directors that the Agency can function, for its expenses in other directions are considerable, and its funds come chiefly from private gifts and donations, of which the greater part are Swiss. In front of the long rows of tables men and women of all ages are silently at work. Some are opening letters which Boy Scouts take out of big linen sacks; others read and annotate the open letters, others classify them. Four men at the end of the table do nothing but take out of the envelopes the stamps which foresighted relatives have included to pay for an answer. Sometimes they find money or a check included also. Here, side by side at the same table are a former Swiss Minister and his three daughters, two stenographers who come to work after their regular hours, students, a missionary back from Africa, and several society women of Geneva. This is real democratic collaboration, and comradeship in service.

What is the general functioning of the Information Service? How can they answer the anguished letters of wives, parents or near relatives who ask what has become of this or that soldier who has been reported as "missing" or "disappeared"? The Agency has two different sources of information; on the one hand the letters of civilians, which give the name, the description, the regiment of the man who has disappeared, and on the other hand the cards sent to the Red Cross by the prisoners, which often contain details as to the fate of their comrades. These documents must be classified, the exact information extracted from them, and this in turn put down on a double series of cards, one to be used to answer the requests of civilian relatives and friends, the other for military information. Lastly, the two series must be collated and compared. After that, the information is verified, and the facts which are considered as certain are underlined in red ink. The Agency can now answer both the relatives and the prisoner, and establish communication between them.

Here, in one of the wings, is a little square office where five stenographers are at work under the direction of a large and active young man. He tells us with a certain pride that he alone in the whole Agency has the duty of announcing to relatives the deaths which have occurred either on the battlefield or in the prison camps. He seems to have a keen sense of his responsibility, and, seeing with what scrupulous care he verifies every detail of his tragic information, we must admit that he is worthy of this heavy duty.

We leave the office of the announcer of death to visit a member of the Executive Committee. He shows us on a blackboard some figures which sum up the activities of the Agency. From September 2, 1939, to August 15, 1940, 950,000 letters had been received, read and classified. 840,000 letters had been sent; 5,000 special inquiries had been made as to soldiers, and 26,000 as to civilians; 600,000 messages from civilians on special postcards had been transmitted in various countries and continents; 63 dockets had been prepared containing more than 8,000,000 cards. The daily mail sometimes brings as many as 60,000 letters, and they must not be allowed to accumulate, for the next day may bring an even larger number, according to the unpredictable developments of a war which is constantly extending to other nations. Since that time, all these figures have of course doubled and trebled.

These numbers are not mere numbers. They represent millions of human agonies. Each of these questions is a cry: Is he alive? Where is he? Is he wounded? Each of these answers brings an immense relief for some family—or else a cruel anguish. Here in the Agency of Prisoners war no longer seems to be a great movement of political forces, or of military powers, nor an opportunity for heroic or passionate acts of prowess. It is the immeasurable tragedy of hundreds of thousands of homes—threatened, mutilated or destroyed. Nothing is more pathetic than these reference cards, on which the red line, drawn carefully by a "voluntary collaborator," registers the fate of a family. Nothing is more moving than these offices, where, to the accompaniment of the noise of a hundred typewriters, two long, groping, and desperate searches—separated by thousands of miles—his from his prison camp; theirs from their home—come together at last to give birth to a message.

The present war has killed fewer men than the last. These 8,000,000 messages, received and sent on by the Agency for Prisoners, are most of them messages of life. They represent millions of homes which find relief from the worst agony. Does not such an accomplishment alone justify the existence of a small neutral country?

XI. SWITZERLAND DURING THE WAR

IN the spring of 1939 the National Exhibition opened at Zurich. These Exhibitions take place every twenty-five years, and the last one had been interrupted by the war of 1914. Those who were superstitious saw an evil omen in the return of the Exhibition, but what the people in general found was an admirable proof of the benefits of federal peace and of the cohesion, firmer than ever, of the three groups which it harmonizes. The many strangers who visited Zurich came away enthusiastic and even amazed; everything was so perfect, so well-finished in those constructions, where the most advanced tendencies of modern art were wedded to the best traditional elements, where imposing effects were never obtained by the "Kolossal" but by an exact proportion of surfaces and volumes. An artificial river allowed visitors to see the whole Exhibition while sitting quietly in a little boat. This river skirted the avenues lined with trees, crossed the esplanades which opened upon the pale blue lake, and wound about among the pavilions, between gleaming machines from the factories of Winterthur, before the displays of sumptuous silks, and under the iridescent vaults of the Palace of Aluminum. The history of Switzerland had been illustrated in frescoes along a high-running road which dominated the whole Exhibition and led to a room entirely bare save for a huge reproduction of the Pact of 1291 and the three Crosses; the Christian Cross, that of the Swiss flag and that of the Red Cross.

On the second of September the water of the river ceased to flow, and the esplanades were empty. In the fields the peasants had handed over their implements to their wives. They had hurried to don their uniforms and gallop off on their horses. The defense of the frontier had been provided for several days earlier by the call to arms of the local troops assigned to that task. In forty-eight hours the entire mobilization was complete, and the first cannon had not yet been fired on the Rhine.

"They say we will fight tonight," the men told each other, as they marched in column along the country roads under a sweltering sun. Only yesterday they were in the factory or the office, yet they carried without grumbling their ninety pounds of equipment. They reached their posts and waited. As we write this they are waiting still.

The hardest test for a modern Army is this prolonged waiting in arms. That was made plain by the rapid collapse of France after eight months of inaction and card-playing in the shelter of the Maginot Line.

To the Federal Council and the Swiss General Staff must be given credit for having foreseen this danger from the first. Every resource was methodically used to bolster up the morale both of the troops and of the civilian population, and also to avoid the innumerable causes of discontent, and therefore of defeatism, which come with a prolonged mobilization. Switzerland had understood that the war of today is a formidable conflict of ideologies and of propaganda. Propaganda is the real "secret weapon" of which there has been so much talk, and it is, therefore, only by forging spiritual arms that the courage and will to use material arms can be given to the nation.

The General Staff organized a special service, called Army and Home, which was given two duties; on the one hand to assure the liaison between the mobilized men and the population, and on the other to keep civic spirit alive among the troops, that is to say to teach them to use their leisure.

To accomplish this latter task the following organization was adopted: a Central Office appointed in each unit of the Army, each division or brigade, a liaison officer who in turn named a responsible officer, lieutenant or non-commissioned officer in each battalion. The Central Office sent to these correspondents lists of civilian or military lecturers, a lending library (in cases of ten or fifty books), mobile theatrical companies and variety shows, radio and moving-picture equipment and, lastly, brief outlines of talks which the officers were to give to the men each week during an interim of their work. Through this organization the High Command was constantly aware of the state of mind of the Army, and of questions such as these which the soldiers were asking: "Why are we neutral?" "Are we strong enough?" "Has Switzerland any real justification for resisting the wave of totalitarianism?" "Can it hold out economically?" It was inevitable that men who were separated from their families and their professions, who were tired and who suffered from the bitter winter should sometimes be troubled by doubts. The outlined talks suggested answers to these questions, reminded the men of the lessons of Swiss history, brought them up to date, and gave concrete arguments with which to meet foreign propaganda.

More, much more was done to reinforce the bond between the Army and the civilian population. In a few months an organization was started whose social and economic importance will probably be seen to be much greater after the war than its creators themselves imagined.

This was the Compensation Fund, which works on the following principle: both the workers and the employers contribute to it, the former paying in three per cent of their earnings, the latter three per cent of the total volume of their business transactions. The resulting sum is distributed to the wives of the soldiers as compensation for the salary which their husbands can no longer earn. This concrete work of social solidarity did more than all the patriotic propaganda to appease discontent. It made the citizens proud of their institutions, and reinforced the morale of the Army as much as a victory could have done. Moreover it suggested possibilities for the future. There is already talk of carrying it on after the war in the form of permanent old age insurance.

It was, therefore, under the best possible conditions, both from the military and the civilian point of view, that Switzerland met the crisis of the spring of 1940, which ended the "phoney war" so abruptly.

In a few days the whole country was transformed into a vast armed camp. Enormous barricades were thrown up everywhere, passersby and automobilists were inspected, a universal hunt for Fifth Columnists was set on foot (hundreds were arrested) and a feverish organization of local guards went on. Everyone expected invasion from one hour to the next. The danger grew as the French forces retreated along the Jura, opening the western frontier to the Germans. What was particularly feared was that the latter would attempt a raid on Lyons through the Swiss plateau. There were many violations of Swiss territory by German planes, and people even talked in cautious phrases of an attempt made to sabotage Swiss aerodromes by the "tourists" who arrived in great numbers at a time on a certain Sunday night. . . .

Tension lessened suddenly with the announcement

of the French request for an armistice. The whole situation was altered. Switzerland could no longer count on any ally if it was invaded. It found itself surrounded and cut off. The "finest army in Europe" had collapsed. Could Switzerland hold out? Was it worth while to continue the crushing effort of national defense?

A few weeks of heavy uneasiness followed. A portion of the press began to alter its tone, to try to find some "better side" to the totalitarian régimes. The people, ashamed of this change of face, had no way of showing their feelings. They received silently, but with amazed indignation, a message from the President of the Confederation, who spoke of "relief" because the struggle between the neighbors of Switzerland was over. . . . A so-called "national" movement was beginning to spread propaganda among the workmen, promising them a new socialism, and asking for anti-semitic measures. . . . But the Army was still resolute.

There was urgent need of a speedy and vigorous reaction. But where was the initiative to come from? Any energetic action on the part of the Government would have been considered by the Axis as a "provocation."

Then it was that a dozen men met secretly at Berne. They were young officers, professors, left-wing syndicalists and right-wing "corporative state" men, writers, business men—all determined to pool their efforts to save the country.

The gravity of the hour brought former adversaries together. Prejudices fell before the extreme peril. Opinion was ready for new solutions. It was important that these solutions should be Swiss and not importations from abroad. It was important to fix clearly what *must* be kept of the Swiss heritage at all costs, and what could be renewed freely, according to ancient custom.

They soon agreed to define the situation as follows:

"First, Switzerland is reduced to its own resources, as it has often been in the course of its history. It will survive this European crisis if it can succeed in surmounting its divisions and in collaborating *in its own way* in the creation of a new order.

"Second, the collapse of French democracy cannot shake our faith in the *federalist* democracy, Christian in spirit, on which Switzerland is based.

"Third, the defense of our independence at all costs and the struggle against defeatism are the urgent tasks of the hour. *Those who doubt the necessity of the possibility of our resistance are traitors.* The unanimous affirmation of our absolute determination to defend ourselves, whatever happens, is our only chance of safety.

"Fourth, there would be no defeatism if every Swiss citizen was fully conscious of the true meaning of

Switzerland as an ideal and a treasure-house of civil liberties, dearly won.

"Fifth, there would be no defeatism if each Swiss citizen saw a possibility of working actively in the direction of needed reforms in the social, economic and political order. One cannot die for Switzerland unless one has reason to live for it.

"Sixth, it is obvious that the needed reforms cannot be brought about in our country in our Federal State either by the Rights alone or by the Lefts alone. The collaboration of all the living groups in the country is necessary.

"Youth today is turning more and more away from political parties to groups which act outside these. . . . Group spirit must replace party spirit."

A League was founded soon afterwards. It was given the name of League of the Gothard, for its first manifesto declared that "The Gothard, natural rampart of Switzerland, heart of Europe and frontier of races, is the great symbol in whose name all the Confederates can unite, in spite of their diversities." This League brought together delegates from almost all existing groups, save the political parties, from the Trades-Unions to the Oxford Group, from the League of the "reliefless" (a group formed for economic struggle) to the Boy Scouts, from the Cooperatives to the Catholic Corporationists.

The first act of the League was to publish a proclamation in eighty newspapers which filled an entire page, and which called upon the people and its leaders to resist at any cost, and to make an effort at collaboration between all classes.

Three sets of manifestoes, published a few days apart, which brought together signatures that had never before been seen side by side, a series of articles, and above all the vigorous personal action of the founders of the League in the Army and in the most varied civilian groups—all this struck public opinion and reawakened confidence.

In several cities delegates of the Workmen's Unions and of the Employer's Associations met under the auspices of the League and adopted a plan of "professional community" proposed by the left-wing unions. At the same time the political parties, alarmed at this competition, formed "communities of labor" in several cantons. There was a sort of political truce.

When the national holiday came, on August 1, it was evident that the fog of defeatism and panic had lifted. The action of a small group of citizens, fully aware of their responsibility, had been enough to clarify public opinion. Nothing is more characteristic of federal patriotism than this almost instant appearance of a center of resistance and of activity at a time when the authorities were paralyzed. Nothing could be more reassuring as to the vitality of Swiss democracy.

Yet the war went on! In fact it grew more and more

present and perceptible to the Swiss, although the cannon on the frontiers were silent. It was obvious first of all by the presence of the interned Allies. Thirty thousand French and Polish soldiers had crossed the Swiss frontiers shortly before the Armistice, escaping from the Germans. They had to be disarmed, fed, lodged. As their stay bid fair to be protracted and it was feared that they might demoralize the villages where they were sheltered, something had to be done to occupy them. They were allowed to work in the fields, and a sort of popular university was organized for them by private means and with the help of the Y.M.C.A., where many were able to continue their studies.

War was evident, too, in more dangerous ways. Several times English airplanes, gone astray, bombarded Lausanne, Geneva, Basel, and Zurich, thinking they were flying over Italian territory. A certain number of people were killed and wounded and a few houses were destroyed. A general blackout was decreed for all Switzerland, which is still in force.

Material restrictions, too, began to weigh heavily on the population. Even before the outbreak of war the prudent Swiss Government had foreseen these difficulties. As early as the spring of 1939, directly after the occupation of Prague, Swiss housewives had each been required individually to lay by stocks sufficient for some months, of various staples such as sugar, macaroni, dried vegetables, rice, and so on. As soon as the mobilization was decreed the free sale of these staples was forbidden, and a system of food cards was established. This allowed the Confederation to gather large reserves. It was thanks to this foresight that the Swiss were able to get through the next winter without famine. One by one the channels of communication were closed. The fall of France and the disorganization which followed prevented the Swiss from bringing goods up from the Mediterranean through the Rhône Valley. A single railway line still connected Switzerland with France near Geneva. By some inexplicable accident a bridge on this line was blown up on October 3. All that was left was Italy and the port of Genoa. Switzerland had obtained the use of Greek boats, but when Greece in turn was attacked all communication by sea was cut off. It was only in the spring of 1941 that Switzerland was able to buy a few ships for herself; they can sometimes be seen in the port of New York, flying the Swiss flag. The tragic events of this year have made the classic joke about the Swiss navy into a reality! [1]

What is the economic condition of Switzerland today, placed as it is in the center of the Axis?

The delay or suppression of the means of international transport and commerce are extremely danger-

[1] As to the joke about the "Swiss Admiral," it had been a fact for some time. Admiral Eberle, who commanded the whole American fleet in 1923, was Swiss by birth, as was Admiral de Steiger, who commanded the Pacific fleet.

ous for a country like Switzerland, which has no raw materials and which is, above all, an exporting concern. The Federal Council, faced with this vital danger, was obliged to adopt a series of "plans" and regulations which were like a sort of war-time "new deal."

There were stocks of provisions on hand, but only enough for a few months, although a long war had been foreseen. Switzerland was in the position of a besieged city which could still occasionally negotiate. A commercial treaty was concluded with Germany in 1940, based on the exchange of a given number of pigs for a number of tons of coal. At the same time Switzerland developed with astonishing rapidity a series of "ersatz" (substitute) industries. From the waste of the city of Zurich a gas has been extracted which replaces automobile gasoline, and a gas developed from wood has been used for the same purpose, as it has been in France. Chemical products (paraldehydes) replace alcohol. But it is in the agricultural field that the greatest effort has been expended. A departmental head of the Bureau of Agriculture, Dr. F. T. Wahlen, has proposed a vast project for increased production, which already in the first few months of its functioning has added 50,000 acres to the surface of Switzerland's productive land, and doubled the wheat-yielding area.

Wheat has been planted in all the parks and public squares of cities. In this way unemployment has decreased and the whole population in the cities, as well as in the country, feels that it is sharing in the common work of national defense, by enabling Switzerland to feed itself and so be independent of its neighbors. It is hard to believe that the soil of Switzerland could yield more than it already did. To accomplish this an immense effort, a mingling of all private initiatives in a national framework, was required. The spirit in which this urgent task has been undertaken is all that can prevent it from turning into a form of state collectivism.

Two facts stand out in the financial situation of Switzerland. In the first place, three billion Swiss francs have been spent on the mobilization since 1939 and three war taxes have been added to those already existing. Since these new fiscal burdens are not enough to meet the expenses of the national defense, the Government wishes to introduce indirect taxes, which until now have been very unpopular in Switzerland.

The cost of living has increased twenty-five per cent since the beginning of the war and restrictions are growing more numerous and heavier every month.

Milk, bread, potatoes, and cheese can still be bought freely, but clothes, shoes, wool, and silk are strictly rationed, and coal is becoming scarce and dear.

The following table shows the monthly ration allowed to each person.[2]

[2] A pound is 453.6 grams. A quart is 9/10 of a liter.

750	grams	of	sugar
250	"	"	rice
500	"	"	starches (noodles, macaroni, etc.)
250	"	"	leguminous vegetables
500	"	"	flour or corn
150	"	"	fat or 1½ liters of oil
300	"	"	butter

Only a country in which there prevails a civic discipline both spontaneous and traditional could hope to meet so difficult a situation without an outbreak of disorder, without becoming fertile soil for foreign propaganda. The Swiss seem to understand what the present alternatives are: collectivist regimentation or voluntary self-discipline. They have chosen the latter.

Politically Swiss opinion has, on the whole, reacted to this state of things with a kind of conscientious moderation, a coolness which is almost Anglo-Saxon, but which has in fact been imposed upon it by circumstances. During the war of 1914 to 1918 the sympathies of Latin Switzerland for the Allies and of Germanic Switzerland for Germany were proclaimed with extreme violence. It was the period of the "gulf" between the two halves of the nation. This time there is no gulf. As far as one can judge from letters and conversations, and read through the very prudence of the newspapers, Swiss opinion is universally anti-Nazi. The effort to reconstruct the "frontist" movement of 1934 to 1935, which was pro-Nazi, was killed at birth by a Federal decree of dissolution. A part of the bourgeoisie seems to have watched with sympathy Marshal Pétain's attempt to set up an authoritarian régime in France. The Left was more cautious. But it is impossible to be sure how many friends the "Free France" movement has in Switzerland. It is equally impossible to say with certainty, proof in hand, that the entire country wants an English victory. Yet it should be noted that the English bombs which were dropped on Swiss cities did not rouse any vigorous indignation, even in the newspapers most favorable to "collaboration." Many Swiss still believe, in spite of British apologies, that those bombs were really dropped by planes from another country. . . .

The Swiss press gives little real information as to the genuine state of mind of the country. Not that it lacks courage or conviction, nor even that it is subject to censorship. But each Swiss editor is fully conscious of the danger which he might bring upon his country if he lightly allowed himself the luxury of publishing his personal opinions on international politics. The Axis is on the watch. The slightest "imprudent" remark is taken up the next day by the important newspapers of Berlin or of Rome and becomes a pretext for violent attacks on Switzerland. The idea of a censorship imposed on newspapers before publication is deeply repugnant to the federal mind. The editors prefer a voluntary but scrupulous and careful reserve. They try to dose out the dispatches of Reuter and the D.N.B. equally, and to give the headlines announcing the victory of one side or the other a strictly impartial size and importance.

In spite of this prudence, in spite of the terseness of the newspaper articles—the number of pages has been cut in half—the Swiss press was eagerly read in non-occupied France, as the only source of information that was favorable to the Allies. For this reason the Vichy government decided last May to forbid its entry. Mussolini had long ago taken a like precaution. As for the Germans, they have no illusions as to Swiss opinion of their present régime. One of their recent expressions of bad temper deserves to be mentioned here; after what we have recalled of Switzerland's pacific role, the accusations of Dr. Goebbels have a savor all their own.

"Little Switzerland has consistently sought to introduce a note of discord in the harmony which we are trying to bring into the concert of Europe. It stands obstinately aloof—without reason or provocation—from the New Order."

The Swiss citizen reads this in his newspaper. He is not astonished by the feverish acrimony of the attack, nor by the courteous tone and content of the editorial comments. He says nothing. He thinks of the Gothard.

XII. THE FEDERAL WAY OF LIFE

SWITZERLAND was born under the sign of the Cross. Switzerland is a crusade, motionless in space but marching on in time, coming from a very long past and showing us a path to the future.

At the end of the "highway" which dominated the Exhibition at Zurich in 1939, stood one of the most magnificent symbols of its destiny that any people has ever found: the Three Crosses, that of the Swiss flag, that of the Red Cross which is its daughter, and the Cross of Christ which is their eternal origin.

Woe to the people that has no symbols, or that no longer understands their meaning! The Swiss have known how to be faithful to their three Crosses, and that is why their nation is still strong.

The Swiss flag was originally that of the canton of Schwytz. The White Cross was the sign of a Christian nation, the red background signified that it was an imperial land. Little by little the name of "Schwytzer" was adopted by all the Confederates, and the flag of the free canton became that of all the Alliance, or "Bund." Thus the national and patriotic symbol of the Swiss recalls their primitive "imperial" mission in the political and military order. In defending their flag the Swiss soldiers first of all defend concretely their State and their liberties, but they also defend the ideal of the Christian Empire, that is to say, of a confederated Europe ruled by the highest spiritual values.

The flag of the Red Cross is an inversion of the preceding: the white background is the color of peace. It is the sign of the universal mission of the Swiss State in the order of humanity, the sign of an active and creative neutrality.

Finally that Cross, which, after passing through the red field and the white field, towers to its full height in the background, is the symbol of sacrifice, of the love of fellow-man, and of obedience to an eternal will which transcends the selfish desires of men and nations and their historic vicissitudes.

All this seems very "romantic" in the eyes of the "realists" of our day, but perhaps the example of Switzerland, of its solidity and its long survival, may bring them to reflect anew as to the true nature of realism. To be realistic is to take into account reality, but the whole of reality; to face facts, yes, but all of the facts. Now here is a fact which this entire book has illustrated: Switzerland, made up of paradoxes, was only able to come into being and to endure through the strength of its federal, humanitarian and Christian ideal. On the plane of material interests, of economic selfishness and racial arrogance, it had no sufficient reason for being. In fact the Confederation had at various periods important reasons for breaking up. It exists only by virtue of what modern "realism" considers non-existent. The "realists" who still doubt the practical and concrete force of a common ideal are actually backward minds. They have not known how to draw from present history its lessons. They still belong to the mentality of those who in the past century knew not how to take anything seriously except money and money-making. To appreciate the whole value of that kind of "realism" we need only see to what it has brought the world; we need only look around us.

But there is another realism—the true one which acknowledges that spiritual and psychological factors, the symbols of communion and the will of man, are more important in history than so-called economic "interests." This is not a phrase destined to flatter religious or humanitarian sentimentality. We are merely describing a fact. It is because the dictators of our day have recognized this fact—although they have made an atrocious use of it—that they have found it so easy to beat the "realists" who began by making fun of them. Here is an example: Hitler has won enormous military victories without gold or financial credit. The "realists" judged this impossible, naïve and romantic. But Hitler has demonstrated by sheer fact that a moral force—even if it is an inferior or a destructive one, such as Nazi fanaticism—can easily overcome nations which are much richer and more populous, but which have no living ideal. It will be objected that it was not a moral force, but tanks and planes that defeated France. Yes, but why did not France, which was much richer than the ruined Reich, secure for itself the necessary planes and tanks? In a way quite different from that of the dictators, needless to say, Switzerland has demonstrated by its existence that moral forces are more *real* and more effective than material interests. By virtue of its ideal of solidarity it has been able to solve the most difficult economic problem; that of maintaining a high standard of living in a country without natural resources. By virtue of its ideal of tolerance and co-operation it has been able to surmount the racial rivalries which have been the cause of most modern wars. Lastly, by virtue of its ideal of liberty it has been able to accept the enormous effort (one quite contrary to its material interests) of keeping an army of half a million men mobilized. In these three cases and in twenty more like them, if Switzerland had been "realistic" in the vulgar sense of the word, it would long since have disappeared. If it still exists, it is because the nation has practiced a very different realism—that which gives its real place to the moral ideal.

No nation is strong without a truly living common ideal. This is the first lesson which we draw from the example of Switzerland.

The second is more particular, and perhaps even more important. It is that an ideal can be truly living and active only in a human community which is not too big. If the Swiss ideal has shown itself to be more effective, in last analysis, than so-called "material interests," it is because Switzerland is a small country.

Let us contrast the Swiss example with that of totalitarianism. In both cases we have nations which are strong because they are bound together by influences of a moral order, and these create a unity beyond that of material interests with their rivalries. But in the case of the totalitarians we deal with *standardized masses* whose bond is, at bottom, an *ideology* that has been taught them, imposed upon them in a few years by a party, introduced by force into their minds by means of exactly the same technique as that used by advertisers on the radio. In Switzerland we find, instead, *diversified groups* whose bond is an *ideal,* intimately approved by each man, slowly evolved from a long tradition, cultivated by a patient and liberal education. Among the totalitarians, tyrannical slogans; in Switzerland an innate civic spirit. There a rigid and uniform framework, imposed from without; here organic structures, deeply rooted in life.

Most of these differences come from the fact that totalitarianism is the régime of large countries, hence of masses, whereas Switzerland is a small country. In a small country, groups can remain alive. In a living group an ideal can remain practical.

Thus the example of Switzerland raises the urgent question of the normal size of a human community. It is a problem which has been tragically overlooked until now, but present events oblige us to face and solve it in one way or another. It seems to us to be absolutely vital for the future of democracy.

Democracy is considered as the régime of liberty. Theoretically, indeed, freedom of speech, of worship, of opposition, and certain economic freedoms are secured under it by law. But here is the capital question: Can this ideal be realized on any scale? What, for instance, does freedom of expression mean practically in a very large democracy? Legally each and every individual has the right to speak and to write. But what is the use of speaking if one is not heard or read? And how can a single voice carry beyond a small group? If such a voice is to be heard in a large nation it must make use of the press and the radio. Even if the press and the radio should allow the individual entire freedom of speech—which is improbable for commercial reasons—they are very costly. Not everyone can afford that luxury. The result is that in too large a democracy the average individual has no means of making use of his legal right of freedom of speech. This right is in fact only a fiction for the vast majority of citizens. It is an abstract possibility which can come to concrete realization only for a very small minority.

Thus the same right, guaranteed by the same law, is real in a small community, but fictitious in a larger one. Democracy being the régime of individual liberties, it can only be effectively exercised in dimensions where individual activity is effective. That is to say, in the dimensions of a group, not of the masses.

From this point of view we do not hesitate to say that Switzerland is actually the only country where the democratic régime had been concretely operative. Elsewhere it is a latent possibility, a hope, perhaps a beneficent illusion; in Switzerland it is a daily fact.

By virtue of its geography, its history, and the constant will of its people, Switzerland has remained a *small* State, founded on the collaboration of divers groups, not on a vast unity of race, language, class or ideology. The régime which is founded on the diversity and harmony of varied groups is called federalism. Federalism is, in our opinion, the only *concrete* realization of the democratic ideal.

But federalism is much more than a political régime. It is a philosophy—a way of life. Its basic doctrine is that of respect for the diversity of vocations and persons. It is a radical anti-imperialism. Its perpetual ambition is union in diversity. This is the exact opposite of the totalitarian ambition. Wherever unity by standardization is sought, even within a democracy, the very bases of the democratic ideal are destroyed, and the bases of totalitarianism are set up. Federalism starts from the original diversity of things and creatures, and never tends to suppress this diversity, but, on the contrary, seeks to make it fertile. In this respect it is the one doctrine that is genuinely realistic, that is to say, in agreement with the laws of nature. For nature itself is anti-totalitarian. Whatever is organic, that is to say, living, is "federalist" in the present wider sense of the term. All that is really human is contrary to uniformization. Marriage, for instance, is a federal union, because it does not presuppose the identity of the conjoined, but is based, on the contrary, on the diversity of the sexes. Painting is a federal art, for it does not obtain harmonies by mixing all the colors together, but, on the contrary, by respecting their particular and complementary qualities. The redder a red is, the better it will bring out the quality of a very green green. (The totalitarian system conceives of "order" only through the suppression of opposites and of individual qualities. It crushes all the colors together, giving a familiar kind of brown. . . .) The human body is a federal structure, because the life of the whole presupposes the autonomy of each organ, and its particular, original and irreplaceable co-operation. What is more "federal" than the blood, in which countless individual cells of different kinds, red and white corpuscles, platelets, each with its own structure and function, co-operate to carry life to all parts of the body?

Thus Switzerland has wedded its different races, created new cultural harmonies, slowly composed a living body of which the twenty-two cantons are the organs, at once autonomous and bound together, and of which an immense number of groups—families, parishes, communes, trades-unions, co-operatives, societies of all kinds, are the cells. In these groups all is still to the measure of man, within reach of the hand, within sound of the voice. In each of these cells every individual can make himself heard, can act with knowledge and see the results of his action, can exercise practically the rights which the law guarantees him.

"The small State," wrote Jakob Burckhardt, "exists that there may be in the world a corner of earth where the greater part of the inhabitants can enjoy the quality of citizenship in the true sense of the word.

"The small State possesses nothing but the real and genuine liberty whereby it fully compensates for the huge advantages and even the power of the big States."

We might add, the little State exists in order that there may be somewhere in the world a human community where thought, where the ideal, *can* become an act.

In fact, the civic achievement of the Helvetian Confederation during six centuries could be characterized as an immense effort to adapt public institutions to the measure of the real man. Man being real, that is to say responsible and effective only within a human group, all this civic effort has consisted in preserving and harmonizing the groups. This is fundamentally an anti-political effort, and as such diametrically opposite to the current of the present century.

Politics have, in fact, become our master-passion. What are politics? Like all passions, they escape definition, they are not what we think, they melt into vague generalities when we attempt to define them, but are all the more terribly effective for their elusiveness. For most men they are first of all a matter of opinion, but that opinion is made by the press, the radio. By whom are these directed, and in what interests? Few know or care to know. Our political opinions, made in series and scarcely modified for individual use, bear on enormous and vague objects, such as "mechanisms of world economics," "will of the people," the "guilt" or "innocence" of nations, "races," "historical necessities" and other entities whose very existence is doubtful. In fact we can form political judgments only when our ignorance grossly simplifies realities and reduces them to some sentimental myth. We can "judge" in this field only when we don't know what we are talking about. That is why political opinions are particularly violent at present; the reduction of human realities to a series of "isms" allows us to take sides without effort, on the strength of words, doctrines, forces—such as marxism, fascism, capitalism—which we do not comprehend.

We talk of "interests" that we have not studied, and that the specialists are not able to define. If precise and definite interests were in question we could come to an understanding, but in the absence of real information, of genuine proofs and measures, the door is opened to the most naïve passions. In Berlin in 1932 it often happened that a Nazi workman would talk to a communist comrade. After a few minutes they would find that they were using the same words, formulating the same grievances. But they only hated each other the more, for each thought: "How can I hate a man so much who says the same things I do? He must be a terribly bad fellow!"

Our era is delirious, and this delirium is called politics. Lost in gigantic masses given over to murderous myths, plaything of powers he cannot see, and by whom he cannot make himself heard, the individual feels himself more despised and helpless than he has ever been in the course of history. He has no hold on the realities or unrealities which determine his life, send him off to war, rouse his passions, demand his sacrifice. Either his opinion is not asked, or he has no way of expressing it. Everything is too big for him, everything escapes him. But if a group is formed somewhere, at once the real world, the human world, takes on again its density, its consistence. It is this freedom-bearing contrast that the spectacle of the Swiss federation offers us.

The President of that League of the Gothard which we mentioned above, wrote us recently: "You ask me to speak to you as a friend, not merely as a political leader. But there is nothing more human than the kind of politics we are making. The justification-for-being of our little country is to save the conception of man, of human dignity, of a real community. All the institutional structures have melted away, and nothing is left but human faces (I am speaking of Switzerland as it is reborn in the League). All that is mass, quantity, anonymity we transform into simple human relationships between man and man. We are recreating *personal politics*."

These words are like a manifesto of the only revolution which could still tempt the men of today: the rise of personal realities against the collectivist myths —of groups against the masses—of the human against the political.

Inevitably it will be objected that this "realism," this practical solidarity, is possible only in a small federal country. "You have yourselves underlined that," it will be said. "The Swiss example is too small to be of any use to a country like America. What could the modern world do with it—this world in which everything seems fated to grow even bigger, out of all proportion: houses, cities, States, super-

States, economics, ways of killing men? Is not the general trend of the age exactly opposite to the federalism that you describe? Are you not being very Utopian?"

To this we have three answers.

The first is that if we want to know exactly what we are talking about when we talk of democracy, of liberty, of tradition, of federal organization, it is in a little State that we must look at the concrete realizations of these words. There only have they remained man-sized, there only can they be understood and verified.

In the second place for those who fear that federalism may be an Utopia we will examine its present chances, as the war is revealing them today.

In 1939 the obstacles to a federal union of European peoples were of two kinds: first, the liberal and capitalistic economy refused to organize and proceed to the repartition of raw materials; and, second, nationalism made the problem of minorities insoluble. But the war will inevitably destroy the bases of the present economy, along with the framework of nationalism. The theoretical possibility of a federation of peoples will thus be constituted, and federalism will appear as the only real alternative to totalitarianism. To individualism and nationalism it will oppose an ideal of co-operation; to the uniform and obligatory collectivism of the totalitarians it will oppose an ideal of union in diversity, of an organic community.

These theoretical possibilities are tempting. Plans are already being made on all sides. Several are worthy of attention: Union Now, Pan-Europa. Their only fault is precisely that they are *plans*. For federalism is never born of theoretical projects. On the contrary, wherever it has existed in a measure—in Switzerland, in the United States, in the British Commonwealth—it has always instinctively set aside systematic solutions proposed or imposed from the center. The existing federations were born of empirical arrangements, of compromises hardly-won through struggle, and often through war.

The federation of peoples if it is to be born will certainly not be a legal construction, but, on the contrary, a process of vivification of already existing roots and centers of different orders, some economic, some religious, some cultural, others geographic. . . .

What are these roots, what are these moral foci of a future federation which are beginning to appear in the present chaos?

Among the people who have been most disappointed by democratic institutions a need of vital liberty still exists. And among the people oppressed by totalitarian institutions a communal feeling is growing up which had ceased to exist in the individualistic democracy. It is the union of these two tendencies which may engender federalism. The federal device brings together paradoxically the "one for all" which defines a community, and the "all for one" which affirms the value of the human person. Moreover, the present war has aggravated the feeling of national differences, but it has also taught the nations to know each other.

To become actuality, federal feeling must have tactics, a technique, and the present war has revealed one. War and revolution have always learned tactics from each other. The French Revolution created the national army, from which Marx got the idea of an organized proletariat. The war of propaganda from 1917-1918 gave Lenin the model for the Russian Revolution, and Hitler, too, refers to it often in *Mein Kampf*. The political term, "front," has been borrowed from the armies. Let us in turn use the tactical lessons of this war for the political revolution which will follow.

The great military lesson of this war, as we have pointed out, is that only federal tactics can be opposed to totalitarian tactics. This admirably illustrates the political reality of our day. It is not the centralized pseudo-democracies which will be able to resist the fascist threat, but the federal democracies. The real antithesis, the only genuinely possible one today is: *federalism* (not democracy in general) versus *totalitarianism*. The fact that this antithesis has shown itself in crude material facts in the test of war should serve as a lesson for future political action.

Henceforth federalism is not an Utopian ideal, nor a result of wishful thinking. It is a vital necessity, a question of life or death for our civilization. The Democracy of tomorrow will be federalist, or it will not be. No other possible alternative exists.

In a centralized State, however "democratic" it may appear, to cut off one or a few governmental heads is enough to make the whole State fall; witness the fate of France. But in a federal democracy, as a Swiss politician has said, you would have as many heads to suppress as there are citizens who care for their concrete liberties, for their commune, their parish, their local roots. This resistance is invincible because it is everywhere, and therefore impossible to grasp. Napoleon, who conquered the great centralized states of his day, was baffled by the two countries, Spain and Russia, in which his armies met with local resistances even though the central power was destroyed.

The tactics of federalism consist first of all in reinforcing now, today, all centers of local resistance. Totalitarianism succeeds only when the masses of a nation have been unified by force. But federal tactics can succeed at once, wherever a center exists, and as soon as a new one develops. Federalism exists wherever a man appears who is fully conscious both of his rights and of his responsibilities. Each of us can be federalist, here and now, in his own field of action. Each of us, in the frame of his own personal life, can transform the "Federal Utopia" into reality. Carrying the military lesson a little further, we might say symbolically that federalism begins wherever a depth appears, wherever superficiality and standardization of tastes and ideas, the precursors of totalitarianism, are rejected and fought, were it only by a single man.

The average man, as we have said, can be truly and concretely himself only in the framework of a local community. These local communities are the living cells of all federations. But a more exacting and complex man can belong to a plurality of such cells. This is the concrete formula of federal liberty, the equivalent of "liberal" tolerance. In each case man can only find his full self-realization in a federal organization of society, because this allows *both* obligation and freedom.

The liberalism of the nineteenth century, because it stressed men's rights rather than their duties, tended to reduce society to what has been aptly called "a dust of individuals." From this dust the dictators found it easy to make their colossus of clay—the State as Idol. The search for an abstract freedom degenerated into a rejection of all obligations as limits on the absolute liberty of the individual. Yet these bonds—family, religion, the home, the soil—are also the roots through which men draw nourishment for their growth.

Individualistic democracy offered only liberty without any concrete pledge or obligation. It fell to pieces at the first onslaught. Fascism and Communism tolerate only obligations, without liberty. They mutilate the human personality. It is only where man wills to be *total* that the State can never be *totalitarian.*

What today prevents men from being entirely human—and even from wanting to be so—is a certain fatalism created by the anarchical development of the machine. Man feels lost in too vast a world. He dares not hope for a return to more normal conditions because he believes that everything is moving inevitably in the direction of even more inhuman giganticism.

To this despairing skepticism, which is widespread, we give our third answer: the malady of the modern world, *giganticism,* is now reaching its crucial phase. It may, of course, go a little further: the great nations may form three or four blocs of States, their wars may become wars of continents, anonymous or dictatorial tyranny may become more implacable, our protests may be of no avail. But already we can foresee the inevitable end of the adventure. These monstrous super-States, these insane concentrations of power can only end in catastrophe. The great States have already destroyed the small ones, but they are condemned in turn to annihilate each other. Their conflicting imperialisms are mutually destructive. In the end, there will be no victor and no vanquished, only ruins everywhere. Then we will have to reconstruct. We will have before us a blank sheet. The peoples will need a new vision. If civilization is to survive this crisis, it will have no alternative but to come back to realities that are to the measure of man. Then the small state will once again be the model and the ideal, as it was in the great eras of western civilization. Then will come the hour of the federal idea, which Switzerland today incarnates.

We can sum up in the following paradoxical formula: the example of Switzerland tends to show the human advantage of what is small over what is huge, and of what is complex over what is arbitrarily simplified.

A real human community must be of limited dimensions. If we expand its limits too far it ceases to be a community, just as a house would cease to be habitable if the size of the rooms, of the stairways, of the furniture was multiplied a hundred times. Since the size of man is fixed and unchangeable, social, political and economic institutions must take it into account; they must not grow irrationally. Socially the institution which is to the measure of man is the family; politically, the commune; economically, the small business. These Switzerland has known how to preserve. But that it has done so has not in the least prevented it from having a wide vision and accomplishing great things in the material and philanthropic order. To attain these results Switzerland did not begin by destroying the small cells: it federated them, little by little, safeguarding their autonomy and their peculiarities. It did not line them up or group them arbitrarily into a pyramidal system around a single center. It worked, like nature, by means of arrangements, adaptations and compromises. Various networks of alliances grew up around several centers, some of them political, some religious or cultural, others economic. This care to respect diversity in union and autonomy in collaboration leads, as we have seen, to a very complicated political organization, and to an economic structure which is partly individualistic, partly centralized. But though it requires much more effort, much more patience and ingenuity than the totalitarian system, that is the price paid for safeguarding the human aspects of life. The totalitarian system, which creates uniformity by dint of rules and regulations, gains a certain material force, but loses what makes the value of life. The modern mania for simplification and for systematizing is the sign of a laziness of mind and of imagination. It is a fatal malady. To live and to give life is never as simple as to kill. Let us not, then, accuse federalism of being "too complicated." It is complicated only in the measure in which it is adapted to living reality, and it has the great advantage of demanding of men an effort which commits and at the same time sustains them.

Can we not imagine federalism of the Swiss type extended to other peoples? True, we have shown that the geographic conditions of Switzerland played a large part in the formation of this régime. But there are certain principles which can be deduced from it that are valid for all countries. The most important of these is the subordination of the central State to local human realities. Let the State, for instance, take charge of large material enterprises, which require a central organization and a collective discipline. That is necessary and reasonable. It is not in the centralization of the postal services or railroads that the danger lies, but in the uniformity imposed on consciences, in the destruction of communities, that is to say, in the centralization of realities which by definition can only exist on a small scale, and are local and personal.

Can we not ask of tomorrow an organization of society which, instead of subordinating everything to material power or to some ideology or *"ism,"* will take the nature of things and the concrete interests of persons into account? Can we not dream of a society which would at last distinguish between what is material and what is human, which would centralize those things that can only function when they are so organized, but in which those things that can only live in their own place and way would be left free and autonomous? Must we call "Utopian" this solution which actually exists in Switzerland, which has proved itself strong for centuries through the most varied epochs, which is, at bottom, good sense itself, and which is, moreover, the only hope left us?

Some people will call this visionary, or at least premature, but if we refuse to imagine a possible day-after-tomorrow we may find ourselves tomorrow aimless and therefore weak, beaten beforehand by the totalitarian Utopias, which know well enough how to make long plans.

It may be that the world of tomorrow will only prolong and aggravate the vices of the present world. In that case—and it is the most probable one—the federal idea will have time to ripen in the consciences of men. The ills of the world will teach its value to mankind much better than could the most persuasive propaganda. Switzerland, which now *lives* this federal solution, will have to be silent and hope to be forgotten for a time. The "little seed" will survive in darkness, as best it can.

But there is something mortal, in the long run, in whatever too much exceeds the capacity of the active and responsible individual—the person. When the world has learned this at its own expense perhaps men may ask of the small countries the secret of a more truly human life.

Switzerland has jealously preserved that secret through the ages. The justification of its existence is that it may keep the knowledge for the future. Will it, according to Victor Hugo's prophecy, "have the last word in history"? We do not know. But what we do know is that somewhere on earth—in the very heart of the European cyclone—exists a hope, strongly defended, which waits its hour. Its name is Switzerland.

INDEX